Daily Skill Builders:
Algebra

By
ANN FISHER

COPYRIGHT © 2008 Mark Twain Media, Inc.

ISBN 978-1-58037-442-2

Printing No. CD-404083

Mark Twain Media, Inc., Publishers
Distributed by Carson-Dellosa Publishing Company, Inc.

Table of Contents

Introduction to the Teacher

Daily Skill Builders: Algebra is a powerful tool that will help you equip your middle school students with a myriad of important algebra skills. Each half-page reproducible activity targets a specific skill, as shown in the Table of Contents. Tied to NCTM standards, these activities provide practice in essential algebraic formats.

Your students will analyze patterns and decipher word problems. They will complete tables and graphs, distinguish between linear and nonlinear functions, and compute ratios and percentages. Students will get lots of practice with slope, *y*-intercept, geometrical patterns, and more.

The activities are grouped into three levels of increasing difficulty. Level One includes problems that are appropriate for upper fifth and sixth graders. Level Two is suitable for students in grades six and seven. Level Three reaches skills for seventh and eighth graders. Your own curriculum, state standards, and students' abilities will determine which sections of the book you will use and when.

At all three levels, exercises are placed from easiest to most difficult. Use the standards-correlation chart in the front of the book to locate problems on a specific skill at a specific level. Please note that many topics and skills overlap among multiple sections of the book.

As students progress through the activities in this book, they will find fewer and fewer instructions. For example, #143 features a rate/time/distance problem about an eating contest. Students are asked to find the winner, but not told how to do that. The learner will need to decide if equations, tables, or graphs will be most helpful to solve the problem.

Students will need graph paper to complete some activities. The use of graphing calculators is optional in this book. The problems can be solved with or without them. Generally, however, calculators will be very helpful with the exercises in levels Two and Three.

Important notes:

- Often equations can be written in more than one way. For example, $3x - y = z$ can also be written as $3x = z + y$, $x = z + \dfrac{y}{3}$ and so on. Usually, only one form of an equation is included in the answer key.

- The symbol • is used to indicate multiplication.

Introduction to the Teacher (cont.)

How to Use this Book

Photocopy the pages that contain activities you want to use. Cut the activities apart and assign one at a time. These exercises have been designed primarily for your students to complete independently. These will support and enhance your math curriculum, and can be used sequentially.

Additionally, the exercises can be used

- as daily warm-ups.

- as "extra credit" for students who finish regular work ahead of others.

- as a diagnostic tool. Since the exercises are very short, you can ask students to complete them before you begin a new unit so that you'll know how much time students may need to spend on each skill.

- as review before testing. Give all of your students, or just the ones who need it most, a quick brush-up on weak areas prior to testing.

- for partner work. Assign pairs to complete an activity together.

- to supplement centers in your room on similar topics.

- as bridge-builders with parents. Send home one activity at a time and ask students to complete the page with a family helper. This is a simple way to involve parents in key skill-building activities.

In short, use these Daily Skill Builders any and every way you can to make the most of all the tools packed inside. Expect your students' algebra skills to grow throughout the year!

NCTM Standards Matrix for Grades 5–8

Activities that incorporate the NCTM standards are listed for each level by number.

Patterns, relationships, and functions			
Student Expectations	**Level One Activities**	**Level Two Activities**	**Level Three Activities**
Represent, analyze, and generalize a variety of patterns with tables, graphs, and symbolic rules	1, 2, 3, 4, 5, 6, 12, 13, 14, 15, 16, 17, 23, 27, 47, 49, 50, 51, 52, 53, 54, 56	57, 58, 59, 60, 61, 62, 63, 64, 65, 66, 71, 74, 76, 77, 78, 80, 81, 82, 90, 92, 93, 107, 108, 111, 112	113, 114, 115, 116, 117, 118, 119, 120, 121, 122, 123, 124, 125, 126, 132, 141, 147, 163, 164, 166
Relate and compare different forms of a representation for a relationship (i.e., use a graph to describe a word problem or table, an equation to describe a table, etc.)	3, 4, 5, 6, 7, 8, 9, 10, 11, 12, 13, 14, 15, 16, 17, 20, 22, 23, 27, 28, 29, 30, 47, 48, 49, 50, 56	61, 62, 63, 64, 65, 67, 68, 69, 70, 71, 72, 73, 74, 75, 76, 77, 78, 80, 81, 82, 87, 88, 90, 93, 94, 95, 96, 107, 108, 110, 111, 112	119, 120, 121, 122, 129, 131, 132, 137, 139, 141, 147, 161, 162, 163, 164, 165, 166
Identify functions as linear or nonlinear and contrast their properties from tables, graphs, or equations	11, 14, 15, 16, 17, 22, 23, 30, 49, 50, 53, 56	74, 76, 77, 78, 79, 80, 81, 82, 108	120, 121, 122, 132, 133, 134, 166
Representation & analysis of mathematical situations and structures using algebraic symbols			
Develop an initial conceptual understanding of different uses of variables	3, 18, 19, 20, 21, 30, 31, 35, 36, 38, 39, 40	68, 71, 79, 80, 89, 91, 95	130, 132
Explore relationships between symbolic expressions and graphs of lines, paying particular attention to the meaning of intercept and slope	17, 22, 23, 24, 56	74, 75, 76, 77, 78, 79, 80, 81, 82, 83, 84, 111	122, 132, 135, 136, 137, 138, 139, 140, 166

NCTM Standards Matrix for Grades 5–8 (cont.)

Representation & analysis of mathematical situations and structures using algebraic symbols (cont.)			
Student Expectations	**Level One Activities**	**Level Two Activities**	**Level Three Activities**
Use symbolic algebra to represent situations and to solve problems, especially those that involve linear relationships	7, 8, 18, 20, 22, 23, 24, 25, 26, 27, 28, 29, 30, 31, 32, 33, 34, 45, 47, 51	65, 67, 74, 76, 78, 81, 82, 85, 86, 87, 88, 89, 90, 91, 92, 94, 95, 99, 100, 101, 102, 103, 104, 105, 106, 109, 110, 111	118, 119, 120, 121, 122, 127, 128, 129, 130, 132, 133, 139, 140, 141, 142, 143, 144, 145, 146, 147, 148, 149, 150, 151, 152, 153, 154, 155, 156, 157, 158, 161, 162, 163, 164, 166
Recognize and generate equivalent forms for simple algebraic expressions and solve linear equations	11, 18, 35, 36, 37, 38, 39, 40, 41, 42, 43, 44, 45, 46, 56	68, 85, 86, 88, 89, 95, 96, 97, 98, 99, 100, 101, 102, 103, 104, 105, 106, 109, 110, 111	118, 119, 120, 121, 122, 127, 128, 129, 130, 139, 140, 141, 142, 143, 144, 145, 146, 147, 148, 149, 150, 151, 152, 153, 154, 155, 156, 157, 158, 161, 162, 163, 164, 165
Use mathematical models to represent & understand quantitative relationships			
Model and solve contextualized problems using various representations, such as graphs, tables, and equations	5, 6, 9, 11, 12, 13, 14, 15, 16, 17, 22, 30, 31, 32, 33, 34, 47, 48, 49, 50, 51, 52, 53, 54, 55, 56	61, 62, 63, 64, 65, 70, 71, 72, 73, 74, 75, 76, 80, 85, 86, 87, 89, 90, 91, 92, 93, 94, 107, 108, 109, 110, 111, 112	119, 120, 123, 124, 125, 126, 129, 130, 131, 132, 141, 142, 143, 144, 147, 148, 159, 160, 161, 162, 163, 164
Analyze change in various contexts			
Use graphs to analyze the nature of changes in quantities in linear relationships	11, 12, 13, 14, 17, 24, 50, 53, 54, 55, 56	73, 74, 75, 76, 77, 78, 79, 80, 81, 82, 93, 107, 108, 111, 112	120, 123, 124, 131, 132, 141

LEVEL ONE

ACTIVITY 1 **Number Patterns**

Name:_____

Date:_____

Study the pattern for each sequence. Find the pattern and the next four numbers.

1. 64, 56, 48, 40, ...

    Describe the pattern for the sequence: _____

    The next four numbers are: _____

2. 7, 7, 14, 42, ...

    Describe the pattern for the sequence: _____

    The next four numbers are: _____

3. 5, 3, 9, 7, 13, ...

    Describe the pattern for the sequence: _____

    The next four numbers are: _____

ACTIVITY 2 **Number Patterns**

Name:_____

Date:_____

Place the given numbers in the diagram so that the sum
along each line is the same magic sum. The sum for each row in the diagram should be the same.

1. Use the digits 12 through 18.
    The 15 is placed for you.

2. Use odd numbers from 7 to 23.
    The 15 is placed for you.

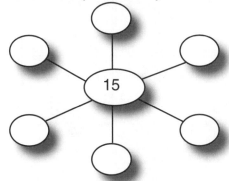

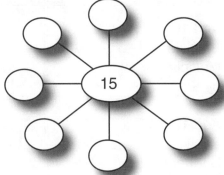

Magic sum _____

Magic sum _____

3. Why do you think the magic sum is the same in both diagrams? _____

    _____

4. Describe the "rule" or pattern for finding the magic sum. _____

    _____

1

ACTIVITY 3 **Number Patterns**

Name:_____

Date:_____

Each table shows a function machine. The first column (*x*)
shows what number goes into the machine. The second column (*y*) shows what number comes out. Figure out the rule each machine uses. Then complete the missing numbers in each one.

1.

x	y
120	20
72	12
6	1
36	
78	
90	

2.

x	y
2	5
4	9
20	41
15	
11	
35	

3.

x	y
5	13
14	40
9	25
12	
20	
25	

Rule: _____

Rule: _____

Rule: _____

Choose the correct equation for each function machine. Write it in the blank below each one.

$2x + 1 = y$ $3x - 2 = y$ $x \div 6 = y$

ACTIVITY 4 **Number Patterns**

Name:_____

Date:_____

Here is a "magical" formula. Try it with 5 different numbers.
Write them in the top line of the chart. Write your answer for each step in the columns.

Pick any number					
Add 10					
Multiply by 5					
Add 1					
Subtract 50					

1. What is the relationship between the first number you used and your final answer?

_____

2. Explain this "magic" formula. Use words or an equation.

_____

ACTIVITY 5 **Number Patterns**

Name: _____

Date: _____

The number of T-shirts sold at Tiny's T-Shirt Shop always follows the same pattern. Complete this bar graph to show the sales pattern during the past four months.

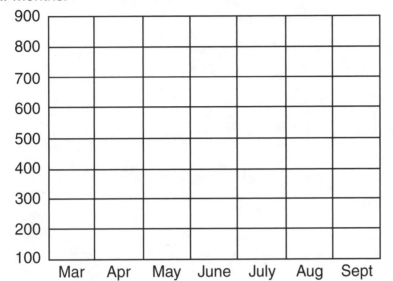

Month	Sales
March	300
April	400
May	500
June	
July	
Aug	
Sept	

Suppose the pattern of sales continues. Show your predictions on the graph and in the chart.

ACTIVITY 6 **Number Patterns**

Name: _____

Date: _____

This rectangle has a perimeter of 26 m.

Length: 8 m

Width: 5 m

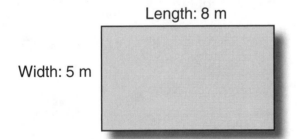

Length (l)	Width (w)	Perimeter (p)
8 m	5 m	26 m
9 m	5 m	**1.**
10 m	5 m	**2.**
11 m	5 m	**3.**

Suppose that width remains the same and the length increases by 1 m. Calculate the new perimeter for the values in the table.

4. Explain the pattern that you see in words. _____

    _____

5. Write the equation for finding the perimeter of a rectangle. _____

6. Write a new equation that explains the pattern. _____

ACTIVITY 7 Word Problems With Equations

Name: _____

Date: _____

Find an equation from the box for each word problem. There is one extra equation.

1. Betsy played her ukulele at a concert. Fans bought 350 tickets for $20 each. How much money came in from ticket sales? _____

2. Betsy charges $350 dollars an hour. She played for 2 hours. Which equation will help you find the amount of money she earned? _____

3. 700 seats are available for Betsy's next concert. If she sells tickets for $20 each, how much money will ticket sales bring in? _____

4. If tickets were $35 this year, and the price goes up by 20% next year, what will be the new price? _____

> **A.** $n = 350 \times 2$
>
> **B.** $700 \times 20 = n$
>
> **C.** $700 \div n = 20$
>
> **D.** $350 \times 20 = n$
>
> **E.** $35 + (35 \times 0.20) = n$

ACTIVITY 8 Word Problems With Equations

Name: _____

Date: _____

Circle the numbers for the two equations that match each word problem.

1. Bryce's gizmo factory yields *x* number of gizmos per day. In the past 20 days, Bryce's factory has produced 240 gizmos. Find the number of gizmos produced per day.

   A. $x + 20 = 240$ **B.** $20x = 240$

   C. $240 - x = 20$ **D.** $240 \div 20 = x$

2. Annie's Antique Mall is open Thursday, Friday, and Saturday each week. Last week, Annie had 360 customers on Thursday and 423 on Friday. If her average number of customers for the week was 450, how many customers did she have on Saturday?

   A. $360 + 423 + 450 = x$ **B.** $450 = (360 + 423 + x) \div 3$

   C. $360 + 423 + x = 450 \cdot 3$ **D.** $450 - (360 + 423) = x$

ACTIVITY 9 Word Problems With Tables

Name:_____

Date:_____

Time period	No. of Minutes	WPM	Number of Words
1–5	5	60	300
6–10	5	57	
7–10	5		
11–15	5		
16–20	5		
21–25	5		
26–30	5		

Mary types at a speed of 60 words per minute. She is able to continue this rate for the first five minutes. However, from 6 to 10 minutes, she loses 3 words per minute. Every five minutes, she loses another 3 words per minute in speed.

Complete this table to figure out how many words Mary types in minutes 26–30.

ACTIVITY 10 Word Problems With Tables

Name:_____

Date:_____

Write a word problem to go with this table. Then give the table a title.

Day	Pepperoni	Cheese
Monday	5	10
Tuesday	6	12
Wednesday	7	14
Thursday	8	16
Friday	9	18

Word Problem: _____

_____

_____

_____

_____

_____

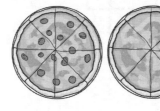

ACTIVITY 11 Word Problems With Graphs

Name:_____

Date:_____

It's spring in Blizzardville, and the snow is finally melting! On April 1, there were 36 inches of snow on the ground. On April 8, there were 34 inches. On April 15, there were 30 inches, on April 22 there were 22 inches, and on April 29, there were just 18 inches of snow left.

Plot the snow remaining on the ground in Blizzardville on this graph. Can you predict ahead of time whether or not you will have a straight line?

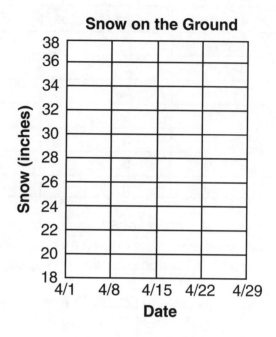

ACTIVITY 12 Word Problems With Graphs

Name:_____

Date:_____

On Mondays, Jada always gets 12 out of 20 words correct from the week's new spelling list. She spells 2 more words correctly each day after that.

1. Which graph goes with this word problem? _____

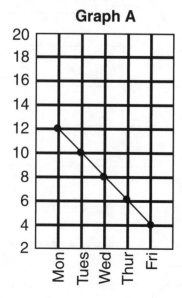

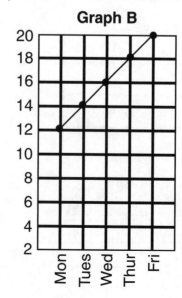

2. Write a word problem for the remaining graph on your own paper.

6

ACTIVITY 13 Word Problems With Tables and Graphs

Name:_____

Date:_____

Kyle makes $7 an hour at a coffee shop. Finish the table, and then finish the graph. Be sure to label each axis with the necessary numbers.

Hours worked	Money earned
0	0
1	7
2	14
3	
4	
5	
6	

Kyle's Coffee Shop Earnings

Money Earned by Kyle

Hours Worked

ACTIVITY 14 Word Problems With Tables and Graphs

Name:_____

Date:_____

A magic vine seed is planted on week 0. In week 1, it grows $\frac{1}{4}$-inch tall. By week 2, its height is $\frac{1}{2}$-inch. Use the graph to finish the table.

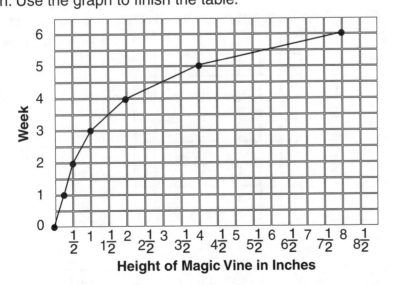

Height of Magic Vine in Inches

Height of Magic Vine

Week	Height (inches)
0	0
1	$\frac{1}{4}$
2	$\frac{1}{2}$
3	
4	

Why does this relationship not produce a straight line? _____

_____

ACTIVITY 15 Linear Relationships

Name:_____

Date:_____

A linear relationship is one in which there is a constant rate of change between two variables. Let's say you save $3 a week from your babysitting job. You will have saved $30 by the end of 10 weeks. This can be shown by the equation $y = 3x$. Make both a table and a graph to illustrate this example. Be sure to label the graph.

Week	Savings
1	$3
2	
3	
4	
5	
6	
7	
8	
9	
10	

Savings From Babysitting Job

Note: A straight line is formed by this *linear* function.

ACTIVITY 16 Linear Relationships

Name:_____

Date:_____

A frightened inchworm is 40 feet off the ground in a tree.
He slowly crawls down. What will his height be after 10 hours? How many hours will it take him to reach the ground? This graph will tell you. Use the information in the graph to complete the table.

1. How many hours does it take the worm to reach the ground?

_____

2. What do you notice about the change in y?

_____

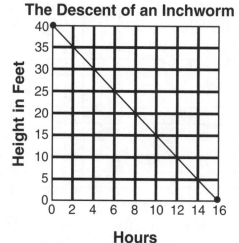

The Descent of an Inchworm

Height in Feet

Hours

Number of hours y	Height in feet x
0	40
2	35
4	
6	
8	20
10	
12	10
14	
16	

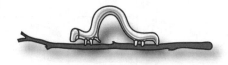

Note: All linear relationships have a constant rate of change.

ACTIVITY 17 Linear Relationships

Name:_____

Date:_____

1. Using what you know about patterns, predict the missing values for *y*
   and write them in the table.

2. Describe a rule to help you determine the value for *y* when you are given *x*.

   _____

   _____

3. Graph the data in the table on a piece of graph paper.

4. Is this a linear function? _____

5. Write an equation that shows the relationship between *x* and *y*.

   _____

x	y
2	
3	
4	
5	14
6	17
7	20
8	
9	26

ACTIVITY 18 Uses of Variables

Name:_____

Date:_____

Sometimes we use variables to express formulas.
To find the perimeter of any square, we use $4S = P$ where *S* is the length of one side and *P* is the perimeter.

Example: 4 x 3 = 12
              The perimeter of the square shown is 12 inches.

Write these four formulas using variables.

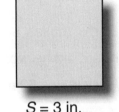

S = 3 in.

1. Area of a rectangle _____

2. Perimeter of rectangle _____

3. Area of a triangle _____

4. Diameter of a circle _____

ACTIVITY 19 Uses of Variables

Name:_____

Date:_____

We use variables when we don't know the numbers.
Here are some fun puzzles that use variables. Find a number that works for each letter. In each problem, one letter represents one number. For example, if you decide that T = 1, throughout that problem, 1 can only be represented by T, and every T will equal 1. Use a different code for each problem.

1.

```
  F O U R
– T W O
─────────
    T W O
```

2.

```
  N I N E
+ S I X
─────────
  F I V E
```

There may be more than one solution.

ACTIVITY 20 Uses of Variables

Name:_____

Date:_____

We use variables to help us find a missing number.
Read each problem. Use a variable to write an equation that would help you solve the problem. (You do not need to solve the equation.)

1. Derek makes $8 an hour. Last week his paycheck was $280, before taxes. How many hours did he work last week? _____

2. Gary drives 60 miles round trip to work. He gets 24 miles from one gallon of gasoline. How many gallons of gas will Gary use driving back and forth to work in a 5-day work week?

    _____

3. A certain patch of mushrooms expands by 3 in.^{2} per hour. If the patch measures 10 in. by 6 in. at 9 A.M., what will be its size at 9 P.M.?

    _____

4. Amy bought a rare teddy bear online for $425. If she marks it up 30% and resells it, how much will she ask for the bear when she sells it?

    _____

ACTIVITY 21 Uses of Variables

Name: _____

Date: _____

In which of these situations will you be required to use a variable to answer the question? Discuss with a classmate, then circle the correct choice.

1. Jill invited 29 people to her dinner party because she can fit exactly that many people in her home. 45% percent replied that they were unable to attend. How many more people should Jill invite now? (variable / no variable)

2. There have been twins in Jan's family, in alternate generations, since 1900. If a generation is every 20 years, how many times were there twins between 2000 and 1900? (variable / no variable)

3. The Balloon Store sold 750 blue and gold balloons for graduation. They sold twice as many blue balloons as gold. How many gold balloons were sold? (variable / no variable)

4. Josh earns $8 an hour. Beth earns $10 an hour. What is the least number of hours each must work before they both earn the same amount of money? (variable / no variable)

5. When Skippy eats his dog food at 6 P.M., he eats 2 cups of food. When he eats at 5 P.M., he eats just $1\frac{1}{2}$ cups of food. If Matt always feeds Skippy at 5 P.M. instead of 6 P.M., in how many days will Matt have saved one quart of dog food? (variable / no variable)

ACTIVITY 22 Equations, Graphs, and Slope

Name: _____

Date: _____

At the shoe factory, one left shoe (x) is made for every right shoe (y). This relationship can be shown in this table:

x	y
1	1
2	
3	
4	
5	

y

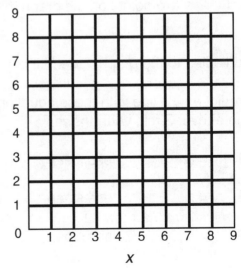

Plot these points on the graph and draw the line that is formed.

This line has a slope of 1, because the change in y is the same as the change in x.

The equation for this line is y = x.

11

ACTIVITY 23 Equations, Graphs, and Slope

Name: _____

Date: _____

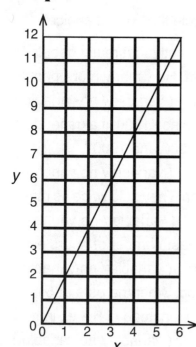

This line has a slope of 2, because the change in y is twice the change in x. Use the line to write a set of 6 points that fall on that line. Begin with:

1. (1, 2)

2. _____

3. _____

4. _____

5. _____

6. _____

The equation for this line is $y =$ _____ .

ACTIVITY 24 Equations, Graphs, and Slope

Name: _____

Date: _____

The equation $y = 4x$ has a slope of 4 because the change in y is four times the change in x.

Plot these two points on the graph that go with this equation.
  (1, 4)   (2, 8)

Add a line to the graph. Extend it beyond the two points.

Predict how a line with these equations would compare to the one above. Circle your answer.

1. $y = 3x$ less steep   same   more steep

2. $y = x$ less steep   same   more steep

3. $y = 5x$ less steep   same   more steep

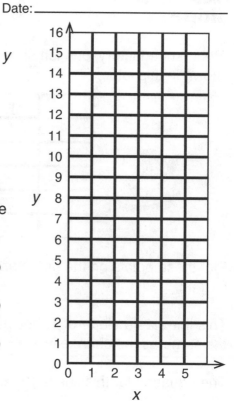

ACTIVITY 25 Multiple-Step Word Problems With Equations

Name: _____

Date: _____

Write an equation for each problem. Then solve it and write the answer. Label your answers with the correct units.

Howard has a ten-gallon hat.

1. How many quarts of ice cream will it hold?

   Equation: _____ Answer: _____

2. How many pints of ice cream will it hold?

   Equation: _____ Answer: _____

3. How many cups of ice cream will it hold?

   Equation: _____ Answer: _____

ACTIVITY 26 Multiple-Step Word Problems With Equations

Name: _____

Date: _____

Write an equation for each problem. Then solve it and write the answer. Be sure to label your answers with the correct units.

1. Petie has a huge ball of pink yarn. If her cat unrolls the whole thing, the yarn will stretch for two miles! How many *yards* of yarn does Petie have?

   Equation: _____ Answer: _____

2. Petie uses all of her pink yarn to crochet 8 baby boots. How many *feet* of yarn are in each baby boot?

   Equation: _____ Answer: _____

3. Petie uses a big ball of blue yarn to make baby hats. She has the same amount of blue yarn as pink yarn. She uses all of the yarn to make three blue hats. How many *inches* of blue yarn are in each hat?

   Equation: _____ Answer: _____

ACTIVITY 27 **Multiple-Step Word Problems With Equations**

Name:_____

Date:_____

Mark Hall sells greeting cards. He earns 30¢ in income for every card he sells to a store. Write an equation that shows the relationship between the number of cards (*C*) Mark sells and his income (*I*). _____

Now use these numbers with your equation to find either Mark's sales or his income for the dates below.

		Number of cards	Income
1.	May 5	60	$18
2.	May 6	142	_____
3.	May 7	_____	$29.70
4.	May 8	435	_____
5.	May 9	_____	$197.40

ACTIVITY 28 **Multiple-Step Word Problems With Equations**

Name:_____

Date:_____

Write a word problem for each equation. Then find the value of *y* in each equation.

1. $15y = 150$ _____

_____

$y =$ _____

2. $30 + y = 150$ _____

_____

$y =$ _____

3. $150 \div 30 = y$ _____

_____

$y =$ _____

ACTIVITY 29 Multiple-Step Word Problems With Equations

Name:_____

Date:_____

Look at this equation: $(2y - 5) + y = 46$

It matches this word problem:

Kelsie has 5 less than twice as many stuffed monkeys as Betsy. Altogether, the girls have 46 stuffed monkeys.

1. What does *y* represent? _____

2. What is the value of *y*? _____

3. How many monkeys does Betsy have? _____
    How many does Kelsie have? _____

ACTIVITY 30 Multiple-Step Word Problems With Equations

Name:_____

Date:_____

Keith is starting his own cleaning service. He spent $240 on a new vacuum and cleaning supplies. For each house he cleans, Keith will charge $85.

# of Houses x	Net Income y
0	-$240
1	**2.**
2	**3.**
3	**4.**
4	**5.**
5	**6.**

1. Write an equation that will help you find the net income Keith will make related to the number of houses he cleans.

_____

Complete this table that shows how much profit Keith will make if he cleans 1, 2, 3, 4 and 5 houses.

7. If you were to plot this table on a grid, would it yield a straight line? _____

8. Why or why not? _____

_____

ACTIVITY 31 Rate/Time/Distance Problems

Name:_____

Date:_____

Write an equation for each word problem, and then solve it.

Note: For all problems, use r = rate of travel, t = time, and d = distance.

1. A car traveling 60 miles per hour will travel 120 miles in 2 hours, 180 miles in 3 hours, and so on. How far will this car travel in 4 hours?

   _____

2. A flock of geese travels 528 miles in 12 hours. What is their rate of travel?

   _____

3. A space shuttle averages 17,222 m.p.h. How far will it travel in one day?

   _____

4. A jet traveled 4,590 miles at a speed of 510 m.p.h. How long did the jet's flight take?

   _____

ACTIVITY 32 Rate/Time/Distance Problems

Name:_____

Date:_____

Write an equation for each word problem, and then solve it.
Note: For all problems here, use r = rate of travel, t = time, and d = distance.

1. A train leaves the station at 9 A.M. traveling at a speed of 90 mph. How far will the train have traveled by noon?

   _____

2. The distance between Chicago and London is 3,960 miles. A pilot leaves Chicago at 3 P.M. and lands in London at 11 P.M. Chicago time. What was his average rate of travel?

   _____

3. The watering hole is 20 miles away. A zebra leaves at 11:00 and runs at 40 mph. A cheetah leaves from the same place at 11:30 and runs at a speed of 70 mph. Which animal gets to the water first? (Hint: An equation may not be necessary.)

   _____

4. The Super Vacuum Cleaner cleans at a speed of 0.2 miles an hour. How many miles of carpeting will it clean in a day?

   _____

ACTIVITY 33 Rate/Time/Distance Problems

Name: _____

Date: _____

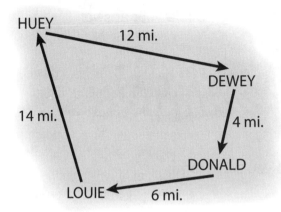

Donald starts out on his moped at 9 A.M. to visit Lou-ie, Huey, and Dewey, in that order. It takes him $\frac{1}{2}$ hour to get to Louie's house and $1\frac{1}{2}$ hours to get to Huey's house. He rides for $1\frac{1}{2}$ hours get to Dewey's. By then, he is ready to get home, and it takes him another $\frac{1}{2}$ hour to do so. What is Donald's average rate of speed?

1. Write an equation that will help you solve the problem.

    _____

2. Solve the equation. Answer: _____

- -

ACTIVITY 34 Rate/Time/Distance Problems

Name: _____

Date: _____

Gary leaves Kalamazoo traveling at a speed of 65 miles per hour, headed for Detroit. He leaves at 9 A.M.

Ann leaves Toledo traveling at just 40 miles per hour.

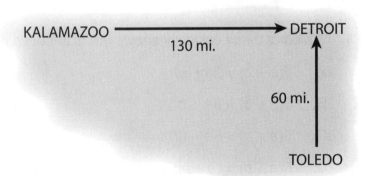

What time should Ann leave Toledo in order to arrive in Detroit at the same time as Gary?

Equation(s): _____

Answer: _____

ACTIVITY 35 Properties and Order of Operations

Name:_____

Date:_____

1. Which property of addition is shown here? $g + h = h + g$ Circle your answer.

   A.   commutative

   B.   associative

   C.   distributive

   D.   all of the above

2. Use the commutative property of addition to help you solve for n.

   A. $36 + 47 = 47 + n$ $n =$ _____

   B. $156 + 10 = 150 + 6 + n$ $n =$ _____

   C. $j + k = k + n$ $n =$ _____

3. Write an equation that shows the associative property of addition.

   _____

- -

ACTIVITY 36 Properties and Order of Operations

Name:_____

Date:_____

1. Which of these correctly shows the distributive property of addition? Circle your answer.

   A. $5(a + b) = 5a \cdot 5b$

   B. $5(a + b) = 5a + b$

   C. $5(a + b) = 5a + 5b$

   D. $5(a + b) = (a + b)5$

2. Write an equation that shows the distributive property of multiplication.

   _____

3. Write an equation that shows the associative property of multiplication.

   _____

ACTIVITY 37 Properties and Order of Operations

Name:_____

Date:_____

In each line, fill in the circle of the letter or letters of the equation(s) that are equivalent to the equation at the beginning of the line.

1. $2(m + n) - 3 = r$ (a.) $2m + 2n - 6 = r$ (b.) $2m + 2n - 3 = r$ (c.) $2m + n - 3 = r$

2. $(J + K) + L = M$ (a.) $J + (K + L) = M$ (b.) $(K + J) + L = M$ (c.) $J + (L + K) = M$

3. $17(c \cdot d) = e$ (a.) $17c + 17d = e$ (b.) $17cd = e$ (c.) $e = 17(c \cdot d)$

4. $(u - v) \cdot w = x$ (a.) $uw - vw = x$ (b.) $w(u - v) = x$ (c.) $uw + vw = x$

5. $5(d + e + 4) = f$ (a.) $5d + e + 4 = f$ (b.) $5d + 5e + 4 = f$ (c.) $5d + 5e + 20 = f$

ACTIVITY 38 Properties and Order of Operations

Name:_____

Date:_____

Evaluate (solve) this equation for Y three times, using the values shown for S and T. Use what you know about the distributive property. Show your work for each step of the equation.

$$3(S + T) = Y$$

1. $S = 4$, $T = 10$

2. $S = \frac{1}{2}$, $T = 6$

3. $S = 1.5$, $T = -3$

ACTIVITY 39 **Properties and Order of** Name:_____

Operations Date:_____

Evaluate (solve) this equation for *Y* three times, using the values shown for *F* and *G*. Use what you know about the distributive property and order of operations. Show your work for each step of the equation.

$$4(F \bullet G - 1) + 5 = Y$$

1. $F = 3$, $G = 2$ **2.** $F = \frac{1}{2}$, $G = 8$ **3.** $F = 20$, $G = 0.5$

_____   _____   _____

ACTIVITY 40 **Properties and Order of** Name:_____

Operations Date:_____

Evaluate (solve) each equation for *n* using the values shown for *a, b,* and *c*. Show your work for each step of the equation. For all equations, $a = 5$, $b = 6$, and $c = 7$.

1. $(2a + 3b) - c = n$ **2.** $n = (5c \div a) \bullet b$ **3.** $(9b - 4c) = n \div a$

_____   _____   _____

ACTIVITY 41 **Properties and Order of** Name:_____
Operations Date:_____

Add operational signs, parentheses, and brackets to make these equations true. Do not change the order of the numbers.

Example: 5   4   7 = 13 ➤ (5 • 4) – 7 = 13

1. 3   18   3 = 18 ➤ _____

2. 5   5   24 = 25 ➤ _____

3. 4   18   2 = 36 ➤ _____

4. 10   5   2 = 0 ➤ _____

5. 120   2   4   10 = 100 ➤ _____

6. 4   3   16   2 = 96 ➤ _____

ACTIVITY 42 **Properties and Order of** Name:_____
Operations Date:_____

Rewrite each equation twice. Change the parentheses, brackets, and operational signs so the answer to each new equation is different.

Example: (9 – 4) • 5 = 25   a. 9 + (4 + 5) = 18   b. (9 • 4) – 5 = 31

1. (72 – 12) • 60 = 360   a. _____   b. _____

2. (7 • 7) – (8 • 3) = 25   a. _____   b. _____

3. 44 ÷ [(4 • 2) + 3] = 4   a. _____   b. _____

4. (10 • 10) + 10 = 110   a. _____   b. _____

5. (5 ÷ 5) • (5 – 5) = 0   a. _____   b. _____

ACTIVITY 43 **Properties and Order of** Name:_____
Operations   Date:_____

Solve these equations. Show each step of your work.

1. $2y - 6 = 12$ **2.** $48 = 3(n \cdot 4)$ **3.** $8n - (9 \cdot 3) = 45$

_____   _____   _____

- -

ACTIVITY 44 **Properties and Order of** Name:_____
Operations   Date:_____

Solve these equations. Show each step of your work.

1. $9n + (5 \div 5) = 1$ **2.** $3n = 42 - (6 \cdot 6)$ **3.** $n + 11 = 3(14 \div 2)$

_____   _____   _____

ACTIVITY 45 Solving Inequalities

Name:_____

Date:_____

1. Harriet is a contestant on TV's *National Idol*. She hopes to get more than half the number of votes from viewers as Sophia, who is the front runner. Sophia has 6,129,000 votes. Write an inequality that will help you find the number of votes Harriet must receive. Then solve.

Inequality: _____ Answer: _____

2. Winslow received less than one-third of the votes that Julius received. If Julius received 2,436,000, how many votes could Winslow have received? Write an inequality that will help you find the number of votes Winslow received. Then solve.

Inequality: _____ Answer: _____

ACTIVITY 46 Solving Inequalities

Name:_____

Date:_____

Solve each inequality for *n*.

1. $n > \frac{1}{2}(14 \cdot 6)$

2. $(476 - 126) \div (42 \div 6) > n$

3. $(55 \div 11) \cdot (\frac{1}{3} \cdot 60) < n$

_____ _____ _____

ACTIVITY 47 More Problems With Tables, Graphs, and Equations

Name:_____

Date:_____

Four toothpicks have been used to make this square.

We can make a second square by adding just three more toothpicks.

Squares	Picks
1	4
2	7
3	
4	
5	
6	
7	
8	
9	
10	

1. Complete the table to find out how many toothpicks are needed to make ten squares.
2. Predict how many toothpicks are needed for:

   15 squares _____   100 squares _____
3. Write an equation that explains this pattern.

   _____

ACTIVITY 48 More Problems With Tables, Graphs, and Equations

Name:_____

Date:_____

Ryan and Reta are collecting nickels and dimes. Every day, Ryan is able to collect 25 nickels while Reta is able to collect just 8 dimes. What are the fewest number of days it will take for Ryan to have at least $3.00 more than Reta? Complete the table to find the answer.

Day	Ryan		Reta		Differ-ence in Value
	# of Nickels	Value of Nickels	# of Dimes	Value of Dimes	
1	25	$1.25	8	$ 0.80	$0.45
2	50				
3	75				
4	100				
5	125				
6	150				
7	175				
8	200				

On what day will Ryan have at least $3.00 more than Reta? _____

ACTIVITY 49 More Problems With Tables, Graphs, and Equations

Name:_____

Date:_____

Here are the first 3 square numbers.

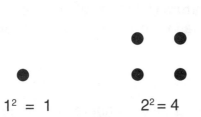

$1^2 = 1$ $2^2 = 4$ $3^2 = 9$

Show these numbers on the graph. Use the original factor as x and the squared number as y. Draw a line to connect these points.

Now, using the line that you've drawn, find an approximate value for the square root of these numbers on the y-axis:

1. 3 _____   **2.** 5 _____   **3.** 7 _____

ACTIVITY 50 More Problems With Tables, Graphs, and Equations

Name:_____

Date:_____

Stock prices for Annie's Antique Company are rising at a steady rate. One share was worth $2 on Monday, and its value increased by $2 every day.

Prices for Zany Zithers stock are falling at a steady rate. One Monday, one share was worth $17. It lost $3 a day throughout the same week.

Make two lines on this graph. Make a solid line that shows the prices for stock in Annie's Antiques. Make a dotted line that shows the prices for Zany Zithers stock. On what day will both stocks sell for the same price? _____

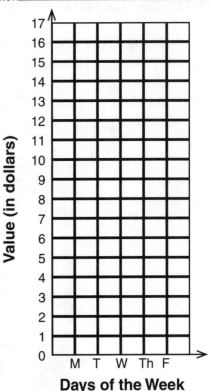

Days of the Week

ACTIVITY 51 More Problems With Tables, Graphs, and Equations

Name:_____

Date:_____

The Jiffy Job Service tests all of its applicants before assigning them to new temporary jobs. Each person must take a typing test. During the test, the applicant types for five minutes. The total number of words (W) are counted. Then the number of errors (E) are subtracted. Finally, the number is divided by 5 (for the 5 minutes). Write an equation to show how this scoring works.

Equation: _____

Now find the typing score for each of these candidates by using their numbers in your equation.

1. Lucy – total words: 325; errors: 10. Equation: _____ Score: _____

2. Ron – total words: 452; errors: 22. Equation: _____ Score: _____

3. Alli – total words: 400; errors: 5. Equation: _____ Score: _____

4. Hank – total words: 433; errors: 13. Equation: _____ Score: _____

ACTIVITY 52 More Problems With Tables, Graphs, and Equations

Name:_____

Date:_____

On this calendar you can see that the first day of the first week is the 1st of the month. The second day of the third week is the 16th, the sixth day of the fourth week is the 27th, and so on.

Can you write an equation that helps you calculate the calendar date (C) when you know the number of the week (W) and the number of the day (D)? _____

FEBRUARY						
1	2	3	4	5	6	7
8	9	10	11	12	13	14
15	16	17	18	19	20	21
22	23	24	25	26	27	28

ACTIVITY 53 Graphs and Linear Relationships

Name:_____

Date:_____

This graph shows the area (in square feet) painted by the Brush Brothers while working on a new mural. Use the graph to answer these questions.

1. How many square feet did the Brush Brothers paint in:
   a.   1 hour _____?
   b.   2 hours _____?
   c.   3 hours _____?
2. What is the rate of increase?

_____

Now extend the line on the graph and then answer the following questions.

3. How many hours will it take the Brothers to paint 50 square feet?

_____

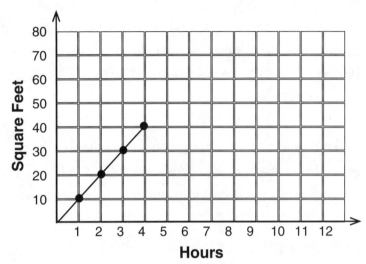

4. How many square feet will they have covered in 12 hours? _____

ACTIVITY 54 Graphs and Linear Relationships

Name:_____

Date:_____

Xylon the alien just loves our fast food. When he eats one Fancy/Appetizing/Tempting Hamburger (or F.A.T.), Xylon gains $2\frac{1}{2}$ pounds. When he eats two F.A.T. burgers, he gains 5 pounds. With just 3 F.A.T. burgers, Xylon gains a whopping $7\frac{1}{2}$ pounds.

Use the graph to plot these points and draw a line that will tell you how many F.A.T. sandwiches Xylon must eat to gain 15 pounds.

_____

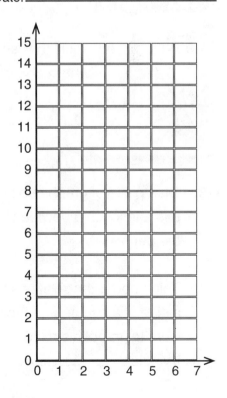

27

ACTIVITY 55 Graphs and Linear Relationships

Name: _____

Date: _____

For years, 20 workers on the assembly line at General Rotors are able to produce 10 rotors per hour. New management decides to increase the number of workers. Five additional workers are added to the line. These 25 workers are expected to produce 15 rotors per hour. When this new plan works successfully, management decides to add 5 more workers. Now these 30 workers are expected to make 20 rotors.

Make a graph of this relationship on your own graph paper. Use x to be the number of workers and y to be the number of rotors. Extend the line to predict how many workers would be needed if management wanted to produce 50 rotors an hour.

How many workers would be needed to make 50 rotors an hour? _____

ACTIVITY 56 Graphs and Linear Relationships

Name: _____

Date: _____

1. Write an equation that shows you how to find the perimeter of an equilateral triangle, where S = length of a side, and P = perimeter. _____

2. Now find the perimeter of this equilateral triangle, using the measurement of the sides shown in the table. Write your answers in the table.

3. On a piece of graph paper, draw the line that shows this relationship between the length of the side and the perimeter.

Length of side	Perimeter
A. 10 feet	
B. 11 feet	
C. 12 feet	
D. 13 feet	

4. Think about the relationship between the length of a side of a square and the perimeter of the square. Make a table on your own paper. If you were to graph this relationship, how would its slope compare to the slope of the line for the triangles? _____

LEVEL TWO

ACTIVITY 57 Number Patterns

Name:_____

Date:_____

Study the pattern for each sequence. Describe the pattern.
Write the missing number in the blank.

1. 1.4   2.8   5.8   _____   3.6   6.6   2.6   5.2

_____

2. 2   3.3   6.6   7.9   _____   17.1   34.2   35.5   71

_____

3. 5   2.5   4.5   9.0   _____   6.5   13.0   6.5   8.5

_____

4. 2.5   3.2   3.9   3.5   _____   3.8   4.5   4.1   3.7

_____

ACTIVITY 58 Number Patterns

Name:_____

Date:_____

1. Describe the relationship between each number and
the two directly above it in the pattern below.

_____

2. Use the relationship you just described to write the next three rows.

Row: 0						1						This pattern is known as
1					1		1					Pascal's triangle.
2				1		2		1				
3			1		3		3		1			
4		1		4		6		4		1		
5	1		5		10		10		5		1	
6	1	6		15		20		15		6		1
7	_____											
8	_____											
9	_____											

ACTIVITY 59 Number Patterns

Name:_____

Date:_____

1. Little Ty is a child prodigy. When he was just two
   years old, he recorded a song he wrote called "Hum." When he was 3, he wrote a song
   called "Chum." When he was 4, he produced the song "Chump." Following this pattern, how
   old do you think Ty was when he recorded "Chumpanzee?" _____

2. Buzzy the Bee flew $\frac{1}{4}$ mile in 3 minutes, $\frac{1}{2}$ mile in 7 minutes, $\frac{3}{4}$ mile in 12 minutes, and 1 mile in 18 minutes. How long will it take Buzzy to fly $1\frac{1}{2}$ miles?

   _____

3. Hank, the furniture mover, can heave 1,200 pounds of furniture an hour during the first
   hour of his work day, from 8 A.M. to 9 A.M. But each hour throughout the day, he can lift
   fewer and fewer pounds. Assuming he has a steady rate of decrease, during his final work
   hour, from 3 P.M. to 4 P.M., he can lift only 360 pounds of furniture an hour. How much less
   furniture does he lift each hour from the previous hour? (Assume he does not take a lunch
   hour.) _____

ACTIVITY 60 Number Patterns

Name:_____

Date:_____

The Proffitt Public Library charges fines on overdue books. Can you figure out the policy? Six
books were all due on April 15, but each one was returned on the date shown and was charged
the fine indicated.

April 17 — 30¢	April 22 — $1.13	May 1 — $3.32
April 21 — 90¢	April 30 — $2.97	May 5 — $4.72

1. What is the policy? _____

   _____

Suppose this policy was applied to books due on May 1st but returned on the dates below.
Write an equation that will tell you the fines for returning books on these dates and solve.

2. May 9 _____

3. May 30 _____

30

ACTIVITY 61 Number Patterns

Name:_____

Date:_____

ReadMore Book Store

DATE	SALES	DATE	SALES
Jan 1	100	Jan 7	250
Jan 2	500	Jan 8	470
Jan 3	150	Jan 9	300
Jan 4	490	Jan 10	460
Jan 5	200	Jan 11	350
Jan 6	480	Jan 12	450

This table shows the number of books sold by two sales clerks, Jan and Jen, at the ReadMore Book Store.

Can you discover the pattern and describe it?

_____

_____

_____

Here is a hint: Jan works on odd-numbered days. Jen works on even-numbered days.

ACTIVITY 62 Number Patterns

Name:_____

Date:_____

This is a timetable for the Gray Dog Bus Company for Tuesday, June 25th.

Timetable for Tuesday June 25th	GRAY DOG BUS CO.			
Bus	Depart from	Departure time	Arrive in	Arrival time
A	Zales	6:00 A.M.	Zithers	6:15 A.M.
B	Yonkers	6:25 A.M.	Yuba	6:45 A.M.
C	Xenia	6:55 A.M.	Xerxes	7:20 A.M.
D		7:30 A.M.		8:00 A.M.
E				
F				

Based on the pattern above, write these cities into the schedule, and then add the departure and arrival times: **Valley, Upton, Umber, Velour, Waverly, Willis.**

ACTIVITY 63   Number Patterns

Name:_____

Date:_____

Study the graph. Which of these statements are true? Circle the number of your answers.

1. The number of meals served increased each day.
2. When there were decreases, the drop was always the same.
3. When there were increases, the rise was always the same.
4. The difference between Sunday and Tuesday is the same as the difference between Tuesday and Thursday.
5. The difference between Sunday and Monday is the same as the difference between Monday and Tuesday.
6. Overall, the number of meals served increased throughout the week.

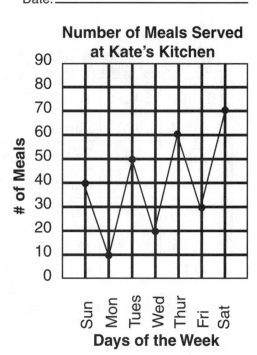

Number of Meals Served at Kate's Kitchen

# of Meals

Days of the Week

ACTIVITY 64   Number Patterns

Name:_____

Date:_____

Which word problem matches the graph?

1. For the first two months of the year, the price of tea decreased 10¢ per pound each month. During the second two months, the price increased 10¢ each month. The next two months, the price went down 10¢ each month. The pattern continued throughout the year.

2. In January, the price of tea was 10¢ per pound higher than in February. In March, the price was 10¢ lower than in February. April, May, and June each saw a 10¢ increase. The next two months each had a 10¢ decrease. After that, the pattern started again with two months of 10¢ increases.

Extend the line to show the price of tea through the end of the year.

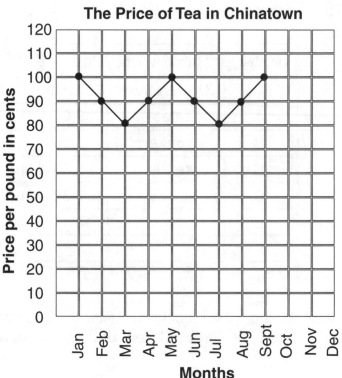

The Price of Tea in Chinatown

Price per pound in cents

Months

ACTIVITY 65 Geometric Patterns

Name:_____

Date:_____

These tiles are in the shape of hexagons. The length of each side is 1 cm.

With one tile, the perimeter is 6 cm.

With two tiles connected, the perimeter is 10 cm.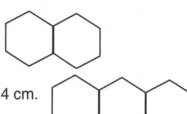

When three tiles are connected, the perimeter is 14 cm.

Make your predictions for the perimeters for each of these lengths:

1. 4 tiles _____
2. 5 tiles _____
3. 10 tiles _____
4. 50 tiles _____
5. What is the pattern? _____
6. Write an equation that shows this pattern. _____

ACTIVITY 66 Geometric Patterns

Name:_____

Date:_____

Look at this line segment.

$$A \qquad B$$

Two points on this line form segment *AB*. Add point *C* to the right of point *B*. With 3 points, you have 3 segments: *AB*, *BC*, and *AC*.

Now add point *D* to the right of *C*. You can make 6 segments with these four points: *AB*, *BC*, *CD*, *AC*, *BD*, and *AD*.

1. Add *E* to the right of *D* and count the segments formed by 5 points. _____
2. Then add *F* to the right of *E* and count the segments formed by 6 points. _____
3. Make a table of your results. Predict the number of segments when you add one more point, point *G* to the right of *F*. _____
4. Predict the number of segments when you add one more point, point *H* to the right of *G*.
    _____
5. What is the pattern? _____

ACTIVITY 67 Word Problems With Equations

Name:_____

Date:_____

Seven Flags Fun Park hires 65 employees at $8.00/hour for 40 hours/week, plus 33 employees at $15/hour for 32 hours/week.

Write the letter of the equation that would help you answer each question. You do not need to solve it. There is one extra equation.

1. How much is the park's weekly payroll?

    _____

2. The park accountant wants to know how much more the park is spending on the $8/hour employees than the $15/hour employees. _____

a.	$(65 \cdot 8 \cdot 40) - (33 \cdot 15 \cdot 32) = n$
b.	$(65 \cdot 40) - (33 \cdot 32) = n$
c.	$(65 \cdot 8 \cdot 40) + (33 \cdot 15 \cdot 32) = n$
d.	$[(65 \cdot 8 \cdot 40) + (33 \cdot 15 \cdot 32)] \times 0.20 = n$
e.	$[(65 \cdot 40) + (33 \cdot 32)] \div 2 = n$

3. What is the average number of hours each employee works? _____

4. If the park management decided to increase the total payroll by 20%, how much would the payroll be? _____

ACTIVITY 68 Word Problems With Equations

Name:_____

Date:_____

Write an equation for each expression. Use *n* for the unknown number.

1. A number that is one-third of the sum of 13 and 23 _____

2. A number when multiplied by one-fourth equals 90 _____

3. Two-tenths of the difference between 65 and 27 _____

4. Fifty-six hundredths divided by three tenths of 8 _____

5. A number that is 9 more than one-half of 32 _____

ACTIVITY 69 Word Problems With Equations

Name:_____

Date:_____

Leif the Lumberjack is clearing a portion of Sherwood Forest so that Robin Hood and his men can build a community for homeless people. He can cut and clear one gigantic tree every 45 minutes. He can clear one medium tree every 30 minutes, and one tiny tree every 15 minutes.

Leif has told Robin that he needs at least 10 hours to clear a certain area. Robin knows the area contains 6 gigantic trees and 8 medium trees. What's the fewest number of tiny trees Leif must cut?

Write an equation for this problem. Then solve. Show your work on the back of this page.

Equation: _____ Answer: _____

ACTIVITY 70 Word Problems With Tables and/or Graphs

Name:_____

Date:_____

Ryan spends more time studying as he gets closer to final exams. Use the information below to complete the table.

1. On Sunday, Ryan spent exactly two hours studying.
2. On Monday, he studied 35 minutes more than on Sunday.
3. On Tuesday, Ryan spent one hour more studying than he had on Sunday.
4. On Wednesday, Ryan spent 20 minutes more than the previous day.
5. Thursday's study time was exactly twice Sunday's time.
6. Friday was just 5 minutes more than Thursday's time.
7. Saturday's time was 10 minutes more than twice Monday's time.

Day of week	Minutes spent studying
Sunday	
Monday	

ACTIVITY 71 Word Problems With Tables and/or Graphs

Name:_____

Date:_____

Complete the table to go with each word problem.

1. The value of *y* is the amount of money in Johnny's piggybank each day. He starts with $42 and takes out 10% each day of the remaining balance for a week. Find out his balance each day, and write that value in *y*.

	y
Day 1	$42
Day 2	
Day 3	
Day 4	
Day 5	
Day 6	
Day 7	

	y
Week 1	$42
Week 2	
Week 3	
Week 4	
Week 5	
Week 6	
Week 7	

2. The value of *y* is the amount of money in Jane's savings account. She begins with $42 dollars and earns 1% simple interest every week on the current balance for seven weeks. Show Jane's total balance for each week in *y*.

ACTIVITY 72 Word Problems With Tables and/or Graphs

Name:_____

Date:_____

This graph shows an irregular decrease in something. Which of these situations could explain this graph? Circle all the ones that might be correct.

1. The daily average temperature in Michigan during one week in November
2. The number of bathing suits left to sell in a gift shop during the last week in June
3. The total number of pages read by a seventh grader in one book for one week
4. The number of Widgets produced at the Widget factory during a week of employee sickness
5. The number of used cars on a sales lot the last week of the month

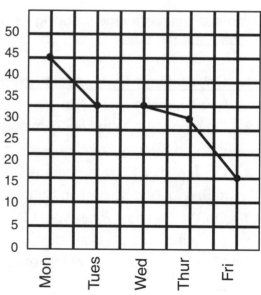

Think of another situation of your own that matches the graph. On the back of this page, write a word problem for it.

ACTIVITY 73 Word Problems With Tables and/or Graphs

Name:_____

Date:_____

A turtle starts a 10-yard race at 1:00. A snail starts the same race at 1:02. At 1:04, the turtle has covered 3 yards, and the snail has covered 2 yards.

Plot two lines on the graph to show the progress of the two animals. Use a solid line for the turtle and a dotted line for the snail. Assume each one continues its current pace throughout the race.

1. Which animal covered 10 yards first?

_____

2. At what time? _____

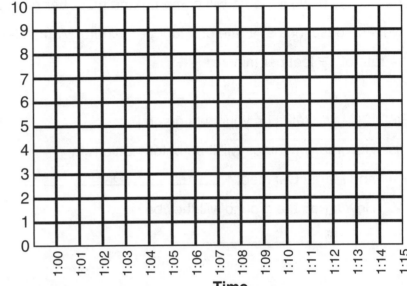

ACTIVITY 74 Word Problems With Tables and/or Graphs

Name:_____

Date:_____

The table shows the perimeter of an equilateral triangle, based on the length of one side. Finish the table. Then graph the results on your own paper. Label each axis with the necessary numbers.

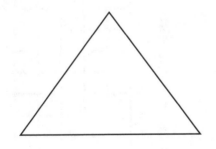

Length of a side (cm)	Perimeter (cm)
0	0
0.75	
1.5	
2.25	
3.0	
3.75	
4.5	

1. What equation helps you find the perimeter? _____

2. Is the change in perimeter constant throughout the table? _____

3. Did your graphing result in a straight line? _____

ACTIVITY 75 Word Problems With Tables and/or Graphs

Name:_____

Date:_____

Little Kitty is 40 feet up in a tree. Bravely, Mama Cat tries to coax her down. Finally, Kitty says she'll come down if Mama will come up and meet her partway. Little Kitty starts at the 40-foot level and descends at a rate of 1 foot per minute. Mama starts at ground level and ascends at the rate of $1\frac{1}{2}$ feet per minute.

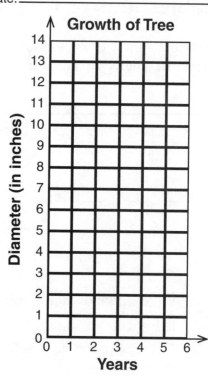

Plot these two rates on your own graph paper.

1. How many minutes will it be before Little Kitty and Mama Cat meet? _____

2. How far off the ground will they be?

    _____

- -

ACTIVITY 76 Linear Relationships

Name:_____

Date:_____

A linear relationship is one in which there is a constant rate of change between two variables. For example, if a tree's diameter grew by 2.2 inches every year, the change would be constant. Complete the table. Then plot a line on the graph to show this relationship.

Years	Diameter
0	0
1	2.2
2	4.4
3	
4	
5	
6	

Growth of Tree

(graph with y-axis "Diameter (in inches)" labeled 0–14 and x-axis "Years" labeled 0–6)

Notice the straight line formed on the graph. Write an equation to show this relationship. Use x for the number of years and y for the tree's diameter. _____

38

ACTIVITY 77   Linear Relationships

Name:_____

Date:_____

Complete the table for each equation. One is a linear
function; the other is not. Predict which one is the linear function. Make a graph for the table you
chose to see whether it is a linear function.

1. $4x - 3 = y$

x	y
1	1
2	
3	
4	
5	
6	

2. $x^2 = y$

x	y
1	1
2	
3	
4	
5	
6	

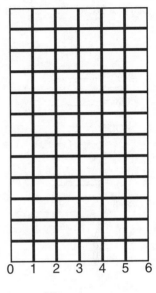

y

0 1 2 3 4 5 6

3. Which equation is linear? _____

ACTIVITY 78   Linear Relationships

Name:_____

Date:_____

Make a table for each equation. Look at the change in y for
each one. Which of these relationships is linear? _____

1. $3x \div 7 = y$

2. $-x \cdot \dfrac{x}{3} = y$

3. $5x \cdot -x = y$

39

ACTIVITY 79 Linear Relationships/ Slope

Name:_____

Date:_____

The slope of a line is the change in *y* over the change in *x*. Change is written as Δ. Find the slope of each of these lines by completing the steps in the box.

1. Δ *y* = _____

   Δ *x* = _____

   Slope = _____

2. Δ *y* = _____

   Δ *x* = _____

   Slope = _____

3. Δ *y* = _____

   Δ *x* = _____

   Slope = _____

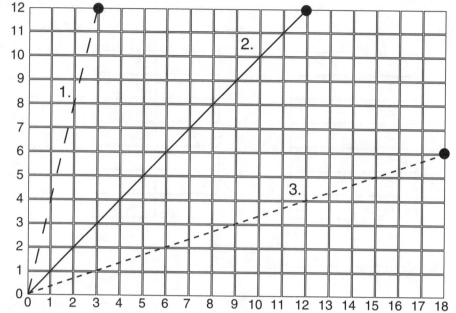

ACTIVITY 80 Linear Relationships/ Slope

Name:_____

Date:_____

1. Complete this table that shows the relationship between the diameter and circumference of a circle. Use 3.14 for pi. **diameter • pi = circumference**

Diameter	Circumference
1	3.14
2	
3	
4	
5	
6	

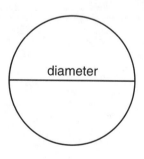

diameter

2. Predict if this is a linear or nonlinear relationship. _____

3. Now on your own graph paper, plot a graph that uses *x* for the diameter and *y* as the circumference.

4. If it is linear, what is the slope of the line you formed? _____

ACTIVITY 81   Linear Relationships/ Slope

Name:_____

Date:_____

1. Finish the table for this equation: $y = 2x - 6$

2. Plot the line on graph paper or a graphing calculator.

3. What is the slope of the line you formed?

   _____

4. Where does the line intercept the y-axis?

   _____

x	y
0	-6
1	
2	
3	
4	
5	

ACTIVITY 82   Slope and "y"-Intercept

Name:_____

Date:_____

1. Finish the table for this equation: $y = x - \dfrac{x}{2}$

2. Plot the line on graph paper or a graphing calculator.

3. Find the slope. _____

4. Where does the line intercept the y-axis?

   _____

x	y
0	
1	
2	
3	
4	
5	
6	

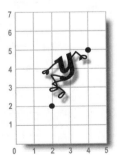

ACTIVITY 83 **Slope and "y"-Intercept** Name:_____

Date:_____

What are the values of slope and *y*-intercept for these lines?

Line	Slope	*y*-intercept
1. $\overleftrightarrow{AB}$	_____	_____
2. $\overleftrightarrow{CD}$	_____	_____
3. $\overleftrightarrow{EF}$	_____	_____

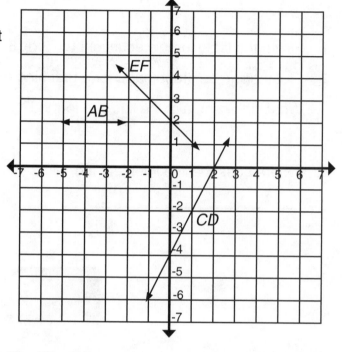

ACTIVITY 84 **Slope and "y"-Intercept** Name:_____

Date:_____

Write the letter of the line on the graph that matches the slope or *y*-intercept listed below.

1.   slope = 1 _____

2.   *y*-intercept = -2 _____

3.   slope = -3 _____

4.   *y*-intercept = 1 _____

5.   slope = 0 _____

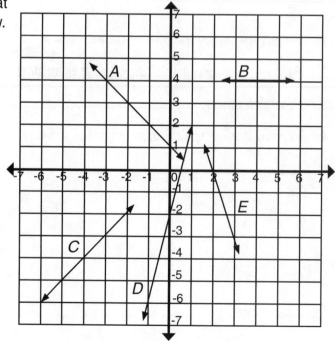

ACTIVITY 85 Multiple-Step Word Problems With Equations

Name:_____

Date:_____

Write an equation for each problem. Then solve.

1. In each 24-hour period, a subway runs a total of 744 miles. On the average, how many miles is this per hour?

    Equation: _____   Answer: _____

2. If a subway runs 440 miles in a 20-hour period, how many *yards* does it average per hour?

    Equation: _____   Answer: _____

3. A model subway at a children's museum travels at a speed of 14 miles per hour. How many *yards* does it travel in two hours?

    Equation: _____   Answer: _____

ACTIVITY 86 Multiple-Step Word Problems With Equations

Name:_____

Date:_____

Write an equation for each problem. Then solve.

1. A regular pentagon has a perimeter of *p*. Find the length of one side, *s*.

    a. Equation: _____
    b. Find *s* if *p* is 4,430: _____
    c. Find *p* if *s* is 34.82: _____

2. A regular heptagon has a perimeter of *h*. Find the combined length of three of its sides, *x*.

    a. Equation: _____
    b. Find *x* if *h* is 3.78: _____
    c. Find *h* if *x* is 4.5: _____

43

ACTIVITY 87 Multiple-Step Word Problems With Equations

Name:_____

Date:_____

1. A theater has 26 rows, with 14 seats in each row. Suppose an aisle is added down the middle of the theater, eliminating two seats from the middle of each row. How many seats are in the auditorium?

   Can you solve this without drawing a picture? Write an equation, then solve.

   Equation: _____   Answer: _____

2. A crowded pet store features two tiers of aquariums along two walls. On one wall of the store, there are 12 aquariums in each tier. On the other wall, there are 19 aquariums in each tier. Suppose after a busy weekend of sales, 9 aquariums are sold from each wall. How many aquariums remain at the end of the weekend?

   Can you solve this without drawing a picture? Write an equation, then solve.

   Equation: _____   Answer: _____

ACTIVITY 88 Multiple-Step Word Problems With Equations

Name:_____

Date:_____

Write an equation for each expression. Solve.

1. 40% of x is 160% of y. Find y if x is 20.

   Equation: _____   Answer: _____

2. Twenty-six more than the square of x is the cube of y. Find x if y is 3.

   Equation: _____   Answer: _____

3. Forty-four less than the cube of x is equal to the square of y. Find y if x is 5.

   Equation: _____   Answer: _____

ACTIVITY 89 Multiple-Step Word Problems With Equations

Name:_____

Date:_____

A pair of $50 jeans is on sale. Each day of the sale, the price is discounted 8% off the original price. Write an equation that will help you find the current price for any day of the sale. Use *p* for the final price. Use *d* for the day of the sale.

Equation: _____

Solve for Day 3 of the sale. Answer: _____

ACTIVITY 90 Multiple-Step Word Problems With Equations

Name:_____

Date:_____

Connie's Construction Company is building a staircase for a customer. Each step rises 6.5″ (height) as it goes forward 8″ (length). Draw a diagram that shows three of these steps with measurements included.

Complete this table to show the total height and length of the staircase after each step is built.

Step	Total height	Total length
1.	6.5	8
2.		
3.		

4. Suppose that the staircase is completed, and the total height plus the total length is 159.5 inches. Write an equation that helps you find the number of steps in the staircase.

Equation: _____   Answer: _____

ACTIVITY 91 Rate/Time/Distance Problems

Name:_____

Date:_____

Write an equation for each word problem, and then solve it. Use the map to answer these questions. For all problems here, use *r* = rate of travel, *t* = time, and *d* = distance

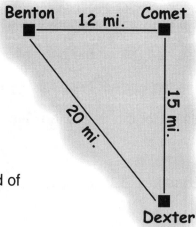

Benton   12 mi.   Comet

20 mi.

15 mi.

Dexter

1. A bus leaves Dexter at 1:00 P.M. and arrives in Comet at 1:20 P.M. What is the rate of speed for the bus?

   Equation: _____

   Answer: _____

2. A bicyclist leaves Benton at 2:00 P.M. and travels at a speed of 15 miles per hour. What time will he arrive in Dexter?

   Equation: _____

   Answer: _____

3. A driver leaves Comet at 6:00 P.M., drives through Dexter, then Benton, and arrives back in Comet at 6:45 P.M. What was his average rate of travel?

   Equation: _____ Answer: _____

ACTIVITY 92 Rate/Time/Distance Problems

Name:_____

Date:_____

The Celery Sellers Sell-Off is on. Here are the top sales speeds of 3 contestants.

Stanley sells 3 pounds of celery per minute. Stella sells 10 pounds of celery every 5 minutes. Stuart sells 15 pounds of celery every 10 minutes.

If the contestants sell at a steady rate for one hour during the contest, how many pounds of celery will each one sell? Hint: First, figure out the rate per minute for each seller.

1. Stanley: _____

2. Stella: _____

3. Stuart: _____

4. Who wins the contest? _____

ACTIVITY 93 Rate/Time/Distance Problems

Name:_____

Date:_____

Two countries are in a space race. Hoosnia launches a rocket at 1 A.M. Its rocket averages a speed of 15,000 mph. Roosnia launches a rocket the same day at 3 A.M. It averages a speed of 20,000 mph. Plot the distance traveled by these two rockets on the graph.

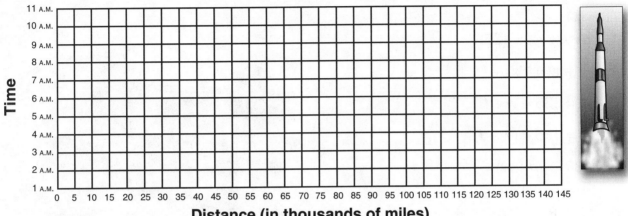

Distance (in thousands of miles)

1. At what time does the Roosnia rocket catch up with the Hoosnia rocket? _____

2. What distance will the two rockets have traveled when their flights intersect? _____

ACTIVITY 94 Rate/Time/Distance Problems

Name:_____

Date:_____

Steam leaves the vent of Factory A and travels at a speed of 15 miles an hour. Steam leaves the vent of Factory B and travels at a speed of 20 miles an hour. It is 30 miles from Factory A to the lake. It is an additional 15 miles from Factory A to Factory B.

Suppose that steam begins leaving both factories at 8 A.M. Which factory's steam reaches the lake first? _____

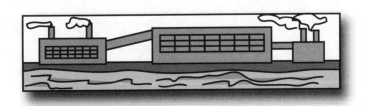

ACTIVITY 95 Equivalent Forms, Properties, and Order of Operations

Name: _____

Date: _____

Jawan worked out for *m* minutes on Monday, *w* minutes on Wednesday, and *f* minutes on Friday. All together, he exercised for 135 minutes on those three days. Circle the number of the equations that match this problem.

1. $m + w + f = 135$

2. $m + w = 135 + f$

3. $m = 135 - w + f$

4. $m = 135 - (w + f)$

5. $135 - (m + w) = f$

ACTIVITY 96 Equivalent Forms, Properties, and Order of Operations

Name: _____

Date: _____

Consider this equation: $2(3x + 4y + 5z) = 100$. Which of these are true about this equation?

1. It is equivalent to this equation: $100 - (3x + 4y) = 5z$

2. It is equivalent to this equation: $3x + 4y + 5x = 50$

3. The value of $3x$ is less than the value of $5z$.

4. $3x + 4y = 50 + 5z$

5. Number **3** may or may not be true.

ACTIVITY 97 Exponents

Name:_____

Date:_____

In each line, fill in the circle of every equation that is equivalent to the equation at the beginning of the line.

1. 10^3
   a. $10 \cdot 3$
   b. $10 \cdot 10 \cdot 10$
   c. $1,000$

2. $3.5 \cdot 10^4$
   a. $3,500$
   b. $3.5 \cdot 10,000$
   c. $35 \cdot 40$

3. $0.0654 \cdot 10^5$
   a. $0.0654 \cdot 100,000$
   b. $65,400$
   c. $6,540$

4. $8,934 \cdot 10^{-2}$
   a. $-893,400$
   b. $8,934 \div 100$
   c. 89.34

5. $10^2 \cdot 10^3$
   a. 10^5
   b. 10^6
   c. $1,000,000$

ACTIVITY 98 Exponents

Name:_____

Date:_____

In each line, fill in the circle of the letter for every equation that is equivalent to the equation at the beginning of the line.

1. $4^2 + 2^3$
   a. $8 + 6$
   b. 24
   c. $24 + 32$

2. $6^2 - 4^3$
   a. $36 - 64$
   b. $43 + 62$
   c. -28

3. $7(x^4 + x^2)$
   a. $7x^6$
   b. $7x^8$
   c. $7x^4 + 7x^2$

4. -4^2
   a. 16
   b. $-4 \cdot 4$
   c. $-4 \cdot -4$

5. $(-3)^3$
   a. -9
   b. $-3 \cdot -3 \cdot -3$
   c. -27

ACTIVITY 99 **Solving Equations**   Name:_____

                                               Date:_____

Solve the following equation using the values shown in each column. Show each step of your work.

$$xy + x$$

1. $x = 5, y = 4$ **2.** $x = 15, y = 60$ **3.** $x = -129, y = 20$

_____   _____   _____

ACTIVITY 100 **Solving Equations**   Name:_____

                                               Date:_____

Solve the following equation using the values shown in each column. Show each step of your work.

$$qr + 6q$$

1. $q = 4, r = \dfrac{1}{2}$ **2.** $q = 1.5, r = 3$ **3.** $q = \dfrac{3}{4}, r = \dfrac{1}{3}$

_____   _____   _____

ACTIVITY 101 **Solving Equations**

Name:_____

Date:_____

Solve the following equation using the values shown in each column. Show each step of your work.

$$(s^2 + t^2) \div u$$

1. $s = 3, t = 4, u = 5$

2. $s = 10, t = 6, u = 8$

3. $s = 11, t = 7, u = -17$

_____   _____   _____

ACTIVITY 102 **Solving Equations**

Name:_____

Date:_____

Solve each equation for n using the values shown for a, b, and c. Show your work for each step of the equation. For all equations, $a = 8$, $b = 6$, and $c = 7$.

1. $(3a + b) \div (c - 1) = n$

2. $2c \left(\frac{a}{2} + \frac{b}{3} \right) = n$

_____   _____

ACTIVITY 103   Solving Equations

Name:_____

Date:_____

Solve these equations. Show each step of your work.

1. $8 \cdot [(42 + 3) \div 5] = n$

2. $[(6 \cdot 7) - 8] + 9 = n$

_____   _____

- -

ACTIVITY 104   Solving Equations

Name:_____

Date:_____

Add operational signs, parentheses, and brackets to make
these equations true. Do not change the order of the numbers.

> **Example:** $5 \quad 4 \quad 7 = 13 \longrightarrow (5 \cdot 4) - 7 = 13$

1. $56 \quad 4^2 \quad 3^2 = 49$

2. $6^3 \quad 6^1 \quad 10^2 = 3{,}600$

3. $25 \quad 15 \quad 10 \quad 8 \quad 7 = 5$

4. $\dfrac{1}{3} \quad \dfrac{1}{4} \quad \dfrac{3}{4} \quad \dfrac{1}{4} = \dfrac{7}{12}$

5. $10^4 \quad 10^2 \quad 10^3 \quad 10^2 \quad = 1{,}100$

ACTIVITY 105   Solving Equations

Name:_____

Date:_____

Add parentheses and brackets to show the order in which
the operations should be carried out. Then solve, showing each step of your work.

1. $n - 5 < 9 \bullet 7 - 6 \div 3$

2. $\frac{1}{2}n + 64 \div 8 - 2 > 10$

_____

_____

ACTIVITY 106   Solving Equations

Name:_____

Date:_____

Solve these equations. Show each step of your work. Give your answer in simplest form.

1. $6 + n > 3 [(4 \bullet 5) - 7]$

2. $\frac{3}{4} \bullet \left[\left(30 \div \frac{6}{2} \right) - \frac{2}{9} \right] > n$

_____

_____

ACTIVITY 107 Advanced Problems With Tables, Graphs, and Equations

Name:_____

Date:_____

The owners of a large auditorium want to divide the room into smaller conference rooms using dividers. These dividers can meet but cannot cross each other. The dividers may run vertically or horizontally.

The diagram shows one such divider that has been added to the auditorium, forming two smaller rooms.

Add a second and third divider (*d*) to the auditorium and count the number of rooms (*r*) created each time.

Plot your results on your own graph paper. Use *d* as the vertical axis. Then use the graph to find the number of dividers needed to make 12 rooms.

Answer: _____

ACTIVITY 108 Advanced Problems With Tables, Graphs, and Equations

Name:_____

Date:_____

The start-up profits of two businesses are shown in the graph. Use the information on the graph to answer these questions.

1. Which business represents a linear relationship? _____
2. What was the best 2-month period for Business B?_____
3. What was the worst 2-month period for Business B?_____

Suppose that for the next 10 months, each business repeats exactly the same course, starting with where they are on the graph at the end of month 10.

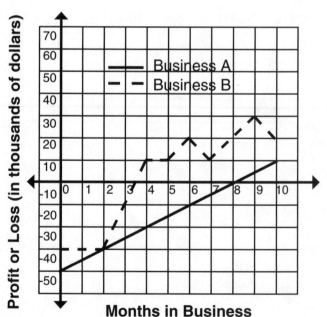

4. What is the profit for business A? _____
5. What is the profit for business B? _____

ACTIVITY 109 Advanced Problems With Tables, Graphs, and Equations

Name:_____

Date:_____

Write an equation for each word problem, then solve.

1. Beth's bank account is paying $6\frac{1}{2}$ % simple interest annually on a balance of $1,000. How much money will she have all together in 5 years?

    Equation: _____

    Answer: _____

2. How many years will it be before Beth earns at least $1,500 in simple interest?

    Equation: _____   Answer: _____

ACTIVITY 110 Advanced Problems With Tables, Graphs, and Equations

Name:_____

Date:_____

A bank robber said to the bank teller, "Give me all your fives, tens, and twenties. But don't give me any fifties or hundreds because those raise suspicion. Also, don't give me more than five grand because if I get caught, the penalties are a lot higher if I have more than that on me."

The bank teller complied. She had 110 twenty dollar bills and 215 ten dollar bills in her drawer. What's the maximum number of five dollar bills she should give the robber?

Write an equation and solve. Show your work.

Equation: _____   Answer: _____

ACTIVITY 111 Advanced Problems With Tables, Graphs, and Equations

Name:_____

Date:_____

Suppose this cube is dipped into a bucket of red paint, covering all the faces of the cube. The cube is then sliced into smaller cubes, each 1 cm x 1 cm x 1 cm (1 cm³).

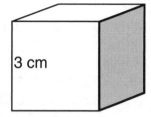

3 cm

Note the table shows how many 1 cm³ cubes are covered with paint on exactly three sides.

Consider the same situation with larger cubes of 4, 5, and 6 cm. Complete the table for those problems as well.

1. Write an equation showing the relationship between columns 1 and 2 of the table.

_____

Length of each side of big cube (s)	Total number of small cubes (c)	Number of cubes with paint on 3 sides (p)
3 cm	27	8
4 cm		
5 cm		
6 cm		

2. Graph the relationship between columns 1 and 3. What is the slope of this line?

_____

ACTIVITY 112 Advanced Problems With Tables, Graphs, and Equations

Name:_____

Date:_____

The boss at the Triangle Factory instructed his workers to produce only triangles with a base and height totaling 32 inches. Some possible combinations are shown in the table below.

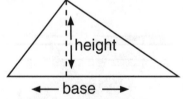

height

base

1. Predict: Will all the triangles have the same area? _____
2. If not, which one will have the largest area? _____
3. Complete the table and check your predictions.

With 1 inch as the smallest possible length for either the height or base of any triangle, write the measurements the boss should use to produce the triangle with

4. The largest possible area: b: _____ h: _____
5. The smallest possible area: b: _____ h: _____
6. On your own paper, graph the relationship between the base of the triangles and the area.

Base (in inches)	Height (in inches)	Area (in sq. in.)
18	14	
20	12	
22	10	
24	8	

LEVEL THREE

ACTIVITY 113 **Number Patterns**

Name:_____

Date:_____

Row: 0						1						
1					1		1					
2				1		2		1				
3			1		3		3		1			
4		1		4		6		4		1		
5	1		5		10		10		5		1	
6	1	6	15	20	15	6	1					
7	1	7	21	35	35	21	7	1				
8	1	8	28	56	70	56	28	8	1			
9	1	9	36	84	126	126	84	36	9	1		
10	1	10	45	120	210	252	210	120	45	10	1	
11	1	11	55	165	330	462	462	330	165	55	11	1

This is a pattern known as Pascal's Triangle.

1. The second number in row five is 5. It is a divisor of every other number in its row (except for the number 1). In what other rows can you find a second number that is a divisor of the other numbers in the row? _____

2. Describe a way to determine, simply by looking at the second number, whether or not the number divides each other number in the row (except for 1) evenly.

_____

ACTIVITY 114 **Number Patterns**

Name:_____

Date:_____

```
                    1
                  1   1
                1   2   1
              1   3   3   1
            1   4   6   4   1
          1   5  10  10   5   1
        1   6  15  20  15   6   1
      1   7  21  35  35  21   7   1
    1   8  28  56  70  56  28   8   1
  1   9  36  84 126 126  84  36   9   1
1  10  45 120 210 252 210 120  45  10   1
```

This is a pattern known as Pascal's Triangle.

Notice that the 1st row (1) and the 4th row (1, 3, 3, 1) contain only odd numbers.

1. What other rows also contain only odd numbers? _____

2. What is the next row that you would expect to contain only odd numbers? _____

3. Describe the pattern that tells you which rows contain only odd numbers.

_____

ACTIVITY 115   Number Patterns

Name:_____

Date:_____

Supply the next three numbers in each pattern.

1. 60, 20, 6$\frac{2}{3}$, 2$\frac{2}{9}$, _____, _____, _____

2. $\frac{1}{8}$, $\frac{1}{4}$, $\frac{3}{4}$, 1$\frac{1}{2}$, 4$\frac{1}{2}$, _____, _____, _____

3. 4.7, 4.8, 5.1, 5.6, _____, _____, _____

4. 10, 9$\frac{1}{2}$, 9$\frac{1}{4}$, 9$\frac{1}{8}$, _____, _____, _____

ACTIVITY 116   Number Patterns

Name:_____

Date:_____

What comes next? Supply the missing numbers in each pattern. Round decimals to two places.

1. 444, 333, 249.75, _____, 140.48, _____

2. 6.5, 8.0, 7.7, _____, 8.9, _____

3. 1, 1, 3, 1.73, _____, 2.24, 7, _____, _____, _____

4. _____, -7.2, 21.6, -64.8, _____, _____

58

ACTIVITY 117 **Number Patterns**

Name:_____

Date:_____

Notice that each number is the sum of the two preceding numbers.

1, 1, 2, 3, 5, 8, 13, 21, 34, 55, 89, 144, 233, 377, 610, 987, ...

You may already know that these numbers are called the Fibonacci sequence.

1. Think of the squares of these numbers. Write the squares of the first 10 Fibonacci numbers.

    _____

2. Write the sum of each pair of consecutive squares, in order from lowest to highest.

    2, 5, 13, _____, _____, _____, _____, _____, _____

3. How do the numbers in **2** compare with those in **1**? _____

    _____

- -

ACTIVITY 118 **Number Patterns**

Name:_____

Date:_____

Notice that each number is the sum of the two preceding numbers.

1, 1, 2, 3, 5, 8, 13, 21, 34, 55, 89, 144, 233, 377, 610, 987, ...

You may already know that these numbers are called the Fibonacci sequence.

1. The letter A is used to identify any number in the sequence. Let n show its place in the series. The sixth number in the series, 8, would be written as A_6. Choose any term in the series (except the first term). Find its square, or A_n^2: _____

2. Find the term that precedes the term you just chose, or $A_{(n-1)}$, and the term that follows it, or $A_{(n+1)}$. Multiply these two numbers. Write the product: _____

3. What is the difference between your two numbers in #2? _____

4. Repeat steps 1–3 for several different terms in the series. What is the result?_____

    _____

5. Write an equation using A_n^2, $A_{(n-1)}$, and $A_{(n+1)}$ that describes what happens. _____

    _____

ACTIVITY 119 Number Patterns

Name: _____

Date: _____

Study this pattern of dots. First count the number of dots in each line. In row 1, there is 1 dot. In row 2, there are 3 dots. In row 3, there are 5 dots.

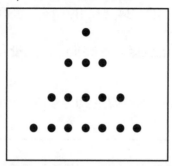

1. How many dots would you expect to see in row 6? _____

Now consider the total number of dots after each new row is added.

2. Suppose there are *n* number of rows. Write an equation that will help you find the total number of dots (*d*). _____

3. How many rows would it take to make a total of 961 dots? _____

ACTIVITY 120 Geometric Patterns

Name: _____

Date: _____

A triangle contains a total of 180°.

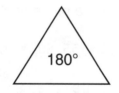

A rectangle contains 360°.

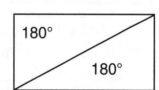

No. of Sides	No. of Degrees
3	180
4	360
5	
6	
7	
8	

On your own paper, draw shapes with the number of sides shown in the table. Divide them into triangles, and then calculate the number of degrees in the entire shape.

1. Write an equation that will help you find the number of degrees (*d*) when you know the number of sides (*s*) of a regular polygon. _____

2. Graph this equation on your own paper. Is this a linear function? _____

ACTIVITY 121   Number Patterns With Tables

Name:_____

Date:_____

Write an equation that explains each table.

x	y
0	3
1	$3\frac{1}{2}$
2	4
3	$4\frac{1}{2}$
4	5

x	y
0	-3
1	$-2\frac{1}{2}$
2	-2
3	$-1\frac{1}{2}$
4	-1

1. _____

Linear? _____

2. _____

Linear? _____

ACTIVITY 122   Number Patterns With Tables

Name:_____

Date:_____

Finish each table. Then write an equation to explain each one.

x	y
-5	-2
-4	-1.5
-3	
-2	
-1	0

x	y
0	0
1	2
2	6
3	
4	20

1. _____

2. _____

3.   Which represents a linear function? _____

ACTIVITY 123 Number Patterns With Graphs

Name:_____

Date:_____

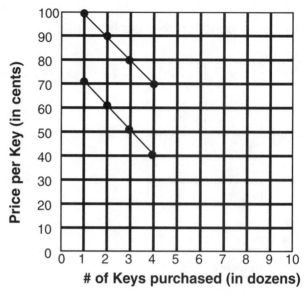

Kevin's Keys sells car keys to auto dealers. Dealers pay $1 per key for the first dozen keys. They pay 90¢ per key for the second dozen, 80¢ per key for the third dozen, and so on. Kate's Keys also sells car keys to auto dealers. They pay 70¢ per key for the first dozen keys, 60¢ per key for the second dozen, and so on. Look at the graph to answer these questions.

Price per Key (in cents)

# of Keys purchased (in dozens)

1. What will a dealer pay per key when he buys his sixth dozen of keys from Kevin? _____

2. What will a dealer pay per key when he buys his fifth dozen of keys from Kate? _____

3. When a dealer buys his first dozen keys from Kate, how much less per key does he pay than if he bought from Kevin? _____

4. If dealer A buys 3 dozen keys from Kevin, and dealer B buys 3 dozen keys from Kate, how much less all together will dealer B pay than dealer A? _____

ACTIVITY 124 Number Patterns With Graphs

Name:_____

Date:_____

Polly's Bags are sold by the thousands to grocery stores. Polly gives different stores different prices, depending on the number of bags each store buys. The more bags a store buys, the better the price per bag. The graph shows the price Polly charges to Stores A, B, and C.

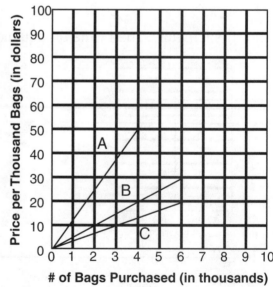

Price per Thousand Bags (in dollars)

# of Bags Purchased (in thousands)

1. Which store buys the most bags? _____
2. Which store buys the least bags? _____
3. Extend all lines. Find the price per thousand bags when each store buys 8,000 bags.

   Store A _____   Store B _____

   Store C _____

4. Look at the difference between what store A pays and what store B pays. Does the difference in price per thousand increase, decrease, or stay the same? _____

62

ACTIVITY 125 **Number Patterns With Graphs**

Name:_____

Date:_____

Loretta's Laundry specializes in washing socks. This graph shows the relationship between the matched pairs of socks that are dropped off and the matched pairs she returns to her customers.

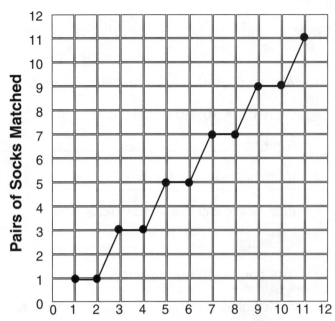

True or False?

1. Even-numbered pairs of socks are matched less frequently than odd numbers of socks. _____

2. Loretta's rate of success matches her increase in laundry. _____

3. Loretta's failure rate matches her increase in laundry. _____

4. 50% of the time, Loretta matched 100% of the socks. _____

5. 50% of the time, Loretta matched 75% of the socks. _____

ACTIVITY 126 **Number Patterns With Graphs**

Name:_____

Date:_____

The chart shows the average daily temperatures for the first 8 months of the year in Predictaville. Extend the pattern, then answer the questions.

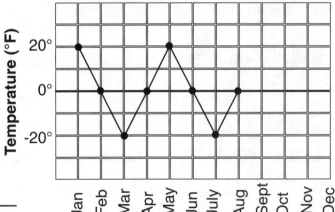

1. What is the rate of change each month? _____

2. What is the highest temperature? _____ How many times a year is that reached? _____

3. What is the lowest temperature? _____ How many times a year is that reached? _____

4. What will be the average temperature for September? _____

5. What will be the average temperature for December? _____

6. What will be the average temperature for the following January? _____

7. What will be the temperature for the following March? _____

8. What is the average yearly temperature in Predictaville? _____

ACTIVITY 127 Word Problems With Equations

Name:_____

Date:_____

Write an equation for each description. Solve.

1. Ann is 27 years less than twice Amy's age. Amy is 28 years older than her daughter, Kelsie, who is 10. How old is Ann?

   Equation: _____   Answer: _____

2. Keith is 3 years older than Dale, who is 5 years more than half of his Uncle Bill's age. Uncle Bill is 84. How old is Keith?

   Equation: _____   Answer: _____

3. The combined age of Sheryl's three daughters is exactly $\frac{1}{2}$ of her own age. Her twins are 6. Her oldest daughter is $\frac{3}{4}$ of the twins' combined ages. How old is Sheryl?

   Equation: _____   Answer: _____

ACTIVITY 128 Word Problems With Equations

Name:_____

Date:_____

Write a word problem for each equation. Then find the value of y in each equation.

1. $\frac{1}{3}(15y - 6) = 150$ _____

   _____ $y =$ _____

2. $32y = 96 \cdot \frac{1}{4} \cdot 52$ _____

   _____ $y =$ _____

3. $[2.95(365 - 30)] \cdot 0.04 = y$ _____

   _____ $y =$ _____

ACTIVITY 129 Word Problems With Equations

Name:_____

Date:_____

A book publisher prints 50 books per year. Can you find out how many total words he prints? Use these facts to write an equation that will tell you.

1. Of the 50 books, 10 are 128 pages long, 10 are 256 pages long, and the rest are 500 pages.
2. In each book, there are 8 blank pages.
3. Each book has 4 pages for Tables of Content and Indexes. These pages have 200 words each.
4. The bodies of the books average 350 words per page.

Equation: _____ Answer: _____

ACTIVITY 130 Word Problems With Equations

Name:_____

Date:_____

Which equation matches each problem? Write the letter in the blank.

a. $\frac{1}{2}n = 16 + \frac{1}{4}(20)$

b. $16 + \frac{1}{4}n = \frac{1}{2}(20)$

c. $\frac{1}{4}n = \frac{1}{2}(20) - 16$

d. $2n = \frac{1}{4}(20) + \frac{1}{2}(16)$

e. $2n = 16 + \frac{1}{4}(20)$

_____ 1. One-fourth of a number is 16 less than $\frac{1}{2}$ of 20.

_____ 2. One-half of a number is 16 more than $\frac{1}{4}$ of 20.

_____ 3. Half of 20 is 16 more than $\frac{1}{4}$ of a number.

_____ 4. Half of 16 and $\frac{1}{4}$ of twenty is twice as big as a number.

_____ 5. Sixteen plus $\frac{1}{4}$ of 20 is twice as big as a number.

ACTIVITY 131   Word Problems With Tables and/or Graphs

Name:_____

Date:_____

Two friends are starting new jobs as truck drivers. Truckin' Tom will drive 3,000 miles every week and earn 42 cents per mile. Drivin' Donna will drive 4,000 miles per week and get paid 35 cents per mile.

1.   In the first week, who makes more money?

     _____

Plot Tom and Donna's earnings for the first 6 weeks on graph paper or on a graphing calculator.

2.   Will the person who makes more during the first week always

     make more? _____

3.   Why or why not? _____

ACTIVITY 132   Word Problems With Tables and/or Graphs

Name:_____

Date:_____

A cylinder's volume can be found using the equation $pi \cdot r^2 \cdot h = v$

Make a table that shows the volume of a cylinder when the radius changes.
Use 3.14 as the value for pi.

radius

r	h	volume
1	10	
2	10	
3	10	
4	10	
5	10	

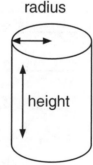

height

Plot this line on graph paper or a graphing calculator. Is this a linear relationship? _____

ACTIVITY 133 Linear Relationships

Name: _____

Date: _____

You may know that linear functions are those in which the rate of change in y is constant. See if you can tell which of these equations represent linear functions without making a graph.

1. $-x \cdot 3 = y$ **a.** linear   **b.** nonlinear

2. $x^2 - 5 = y$ **a.** linear   **b.** nonlinear

3. $5x - 6x = y$ **a.** linear   **b.** nonlinear

4. $y = \frac{1}{4}x + 3$ **a.** linear   **b.** nonlinear

5. $-2x + 8 = y$ **a.** linear   **b.** nonlinear

ACTIVITY 134 Linear Relationships

Name: _____

Date: _____

Read these word problems. Predict if the relationship being described is linear or nonlinear.

1. An ant finds a bread crumb to carry back to his anthill. He walks 9 feet in one minute. Then he walks another 9 feet in the second minute, and another 9 feet in the third minute.

     a. linear   **b.** nonlinear

2. The value of a new car depreciates quickly. In the first year, the value drops by 15%. In the second year, it drops another 10%. In the third year, the value decreases by an additional 7%.

     a. linear   **b.** nonlinear

3. Penny is painting several rooms inside a house. The total area to be painted is 2,000 square feet. After 1 hour of work, Penny has 1,400 square feet left to paint. After 2 hours of work, she has 1,000 sq. ft. to paint. After 3 hours, Penny still needs to paint 650 sq. ft.

     a. linear   **b.** nonlinear

Write two of your own word problems on your own paper. Write one that describes a linear relationship and one that describes a nonlinear relationship.

ACTIVITY 135　Equations, Graphs, and Slope

Name:_____

Date:_____

Describe the segments in this shape.

	slope	y-intercept
1. Left diagonal	_____	_____
2. Right diagonal	_____	_____
3. Horizontal line	_____	_____

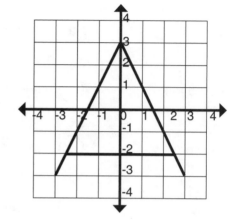

ACTIVITY 136　Equations, Graphs, and Slope

Name:_____

Date:_____

Tell the slope and y-intercept for each equation, without plotting the points.

	slope	y-intercept
1. $y = 6x - 3$	_____	_____
2. $y = \frac{1}{2}x + 2$	_____	_____
3. $y = 4x$	_____	_____
4. $2y = 5x - 4$	_____	_____
5. $\frac{1}{2}y = 3 + x$	_____	_____

ACTIVITY 137   Equations, Slope, and "y"-Intercept

Name:_____

Date:_____

Which line matches each equation?

1. $y = \frac{1}{3}x$ _____

2. $x = -3$ _____

3. $y = x - 3$ _____

4. $y = 3$ _____

5. $y = -x - 3$ _____

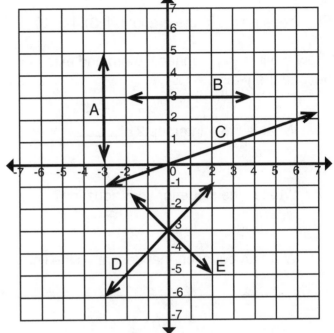

ACTIVITY 138   Equations, Slope, and "y"-Intercept

Name:_____

Date:_____

Place these segments on the graph.

• A segment with a *y*-intercept of 2 and a slope of -1; it should start at the *y*-axis and end at *x* = 2.

• A segment with a *y*-intercept of 2 and a slope of 1; it should start at the *y*-axis and end at *x* = -2.

• A segment with an undefined slope where *x* = 0; it should begin where the other segments begin and end at *y* = -3.

What shape have you made?

_____

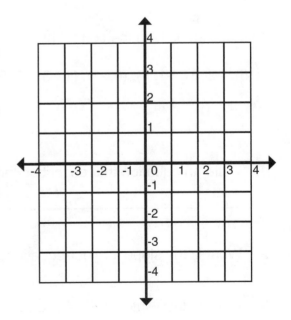

ACTIVITY 139 Equations, Slope, and "y"-Intercept

Name:_____

Date:_____

Plot these points in the graph: (-4, 3), (-2, 2).

Draw the line that connects them and extend it beyond the *y*-axis.

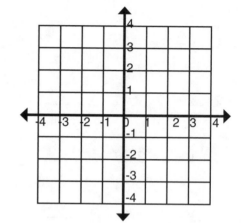

1. What is the *y*-intercept? _____

2. What is the slope for your equation? _____

3. Write an equation that describes the line.

_____

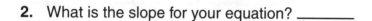

ACTIVITY 140 Equations, Slope, and "y"-Intercept

Name:_____

Date:_____

Write these points in the correct places in a table.

(-3, 5), (-2, 3), (-1, 1), (0, -1), (1, -3), (2, 5)

x	y

1. Write an equation that describes the function of the table.

_____

2. What is the slope for your equation? _____

3. What is the *y*-intercept? _____

ACTIVITY 141 Rate/Time/Distance Problems

Name:_____

Date:_____

The crook leaves the store at 1 A.M., traveling at 60 miles an hour. A state policeman chases the crook. The cop leaves the same store at 1:05, traveling at 70 miles an hour. He must catch the crook before he crosses the state boundary line, which is only 20 miles away.

```
 ┌────────────────────────┊───┐
 │  △                     ┊   │
 │  │ │ store             ┊   │
 │  └─┘                   ┊   │
 │    ───────────────▶    ┊   │
 │        20 miles        ┊   │
 └────────────────────────┊───┘
```

Who gets to the border first? _____

Solve using equations or a graph.

ACTIVITY 142 Rate/Time/Distance Problems

Name:_____

Date:_____

This diagram shows the path of three animals to the pond.

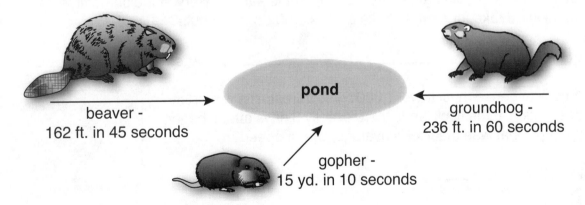

beaver -
162 ft. in 45 seconds

pond

groundhog -
236 ft. in 60 seconds

gopher -
15 yd. in 10 seconds

1. Which animal is traveling the fastest? _____

2. Which animal is traveling the slowest? _____

3. What is the average speed of all 3 animals? _____

ACTIVITY 143 Rate/Time/Distance Problems

Name:_____

Date:_____

The Eggplant Eaters Championship Eat-Off is on.
Here are the top contenders, along with their eating speeds:

Edna eats 14 pints of cooked eggplant every hour.

Egbert eats 3 cups of cooked eggplant every three minutes.

Essie eats 1 quart of cooked eggplant every ten minutes.

The eating contest lasts for 15 minutes.

1. How much does everyone eat?

   a. Edna _____   **b.** Egbert _____   **c.** Essie _____

2. Who is the winner? _____

ACTIVITY 144 Rate/Time/Distance Problems

Name:_____

Date:_____

1. A new baker bakes 5 dozen donuts per hour. An experienced baker bakes 8 dozen do-nuts per hour. If both bakers are working at the same bakery at the same time, how many hours will it take for them to bake at least 100 dozen donuts?

   Equation: _____   Answer: _____

2. A flock of geese must travel 1,000 miles to reach its wintertime destination. If the flock lands there exactly 3 days after it began the trip, what was the flock's average rate of speed?

   Equation: _____

   Answer: _____

3. An ambulance must reach a hospital 9 miles away in less than 10 minutes. How fast must the ambulance travel?

   Equation: _____   Answer: _____

ACTIVITY 145 **Ratios and Proportions** Name:_____

Date:_____

Solve each proportion for x.

1. $\dfrac{16}{5} = \dfrac{8}{x}$ x = _____

2. $\dfrac{90}{36} = \dfrac{x}{54}$ x = _____

3. $\dfrac{7}{8} = \dfrac{x}{6}$ x = _____

4. $\dfrac{x}{15} = \dfrac{9}{10}$ x = _____

5. $\dfrac{10}{9} = \dfrac{6}{x}$ x = _____

6. $\dfrac{15}{25} = \dfrac{x}{20}$ x = _____

ACTIVITY 146 **Ratios and Proportions** Name:_____

Date:_____

1. If 1,200 pencils can be purchased for $24, what would be the price to buy just 800?

_____

2. It takes $3\frac{1}{2}$ pounds of grass seed to plant 4 acres of land. How many pounds of seed are required to plant 25 acres? _____

3. A produce manager is trying to maintain a ratio of 5 bananas for every 3 apples to sell in his market. The stocker tells him he has 265 bananas. How many apples should he have? _____

ACTIVITY 147 Ratios and Proportions

Name:_____

Date:_____

The Pythagorean Theorem says that in a right triangle,
$a^2 + b^2 = c^2$

We know that this triangle exists: $a = 3$, $b = 4$, $c = 5$
because $3^2 + 4^2 = 5^2$.

Use the Pythagorean Theorem to generate the lengths of the sides of three new right triangles. Show your work.

1. $a = 6$, $b = 8$, $c = ?$

2. $a = ?$, $b = 7$, $c = 8\frac{3}{4}$

3. $a = 7\frac{1}{2}$, $b = ?$, $c = 12\frac{1}{2}$

_____ _____ _____

ACTIVITY 148 Ratios and Proportions

Name:_____

Date:_____

A certain alloy requires 3 parts aluminum to 2 parts nickel and 5 parts iron. A manufacturer wants to produce 250 pounds of this alloy. How many pounds of each metal will he need? Write the proportion needed to answer each question. Solve.

1. aluminum   Proportion: _____   Answer: _____

2. nickel   Proportion: _____   Answer: _____

3. iron   Proportion: _____   Answer: _____

Another alloy requires 6 parts aluminum to 4.5 parts nickel and 7 parts iron. How many pounds of each metal are needed to produce 350 pounds of this material?

4. aluminum   Proportion: _____   Answer: _____

5. nickel   Proportion: _____   Answer: _____

6. iron   Proportion: _____   Answer: _____

ACTIVITY 149 · Exponents

Name: _____

Date: _____

True or false? If false, correct the expression.

1. $x^m \div x^n = x^{m-n}$ _____ _____

2. $x^{-n} = \dfrac{1}{x^n}$ _____ _____

3. $-x^2 = (-x)^2$ _____ _____

4. $x^m \cdot x^n = x^{m+n}$ _____ _____

5. $(xy)^5 = x^5 + y^5$ _____ _____

6. $(x^3)^5 = x^8$ _____ _____

ACTIVITY 150 · Exponents

Name: _____

Date: _____

In each line, fill in the circle of the letter for every expression that is equivalent to the expression at the beginning of the line.

1. $(5 \cdot 7)^5$ **a.** $5^5 + 7^5$ **b.** $5^5 \cdot 7^5$ **c.** 35^5

2. $(4^6 \div 4^4)$ **a.** 4^{6-4} **b.** $(4 \div 4)^2$ **c.** $\dfrac{4 \cdot 4 \cdot 4 \cdot 4 \cdot 4 \cdot 4}{4 \cdot 4 \cdot 4 \cdot 4}$

3. $5^2 + 5^3$ **a.** 5^{2+3} **b.** $(5 \cdot 5) + (5 \cdot 5 \cdot 5)$ **c.** $3{,}125$

4. $6^0 \cdot 6^4$ **a.** 0 **b.** $1{,}296$ **c.** $7{,}776$

5. 3^{-4} **a.** $\dfrac{1}{3^4}$ **b.** -81 **c.** $\dfrac{1}{81}$

ACTIVITY 151 Exponents

Name:_____

Date:_____

Add these numbers as exponents in the boxes so each equation is true.

0, 1, 2, 3, 4, 5, 6, 7

Use each number exactly once.

1. $5^{\square} + 4^{\square} = 69$

2. $-(3^{\square}) \cdot 2^{\square} = -144$

3. $10^{\square} \div 10^{\square} = 100$

4. $2^{\square} - 2^{\square} = 63$

ACTIVITY 152 Exponents

Name:_____

Date:_____

Solve each equation.

1. $-(5^2) - 3^1 + 4^2 = $ _____

2. $-(6^2) - (-2)^2 = $ _____

3. $3^5 - (-4)^2 - 6^0 = $ _____

4. $\dfrac{1}{5^3} = $ _____

5. $4^{-3} = $ _____

ACTIVITY 153 Solving Equations

Name:_____

Date:_____

Add operational signs, parentheses, and brackets to make these equations true. Do not change the order of the numbers.

Example: 5   4   7 = 13 ⟶ (5 x 4) − 7 = 13

1. $-(3^2)$ 5 4^2 = -29

2. $\frac{2}{3}$ 4^{-2} 2^2 $= \frac{1}{6}$

3. $\sqrt[3]{27}$ $\sqrt[3]{8}$ $\sqrt[3]{1}$ $= 4\frac{1}{2}$

4. $\sqrt[3]{125}$ $\sqrt{121}$ $\sqrt{81}$ 5   = 10

5. $\sqrt[3]{1,000}$ $\sqrt{144}$ 2^3 5   = 40

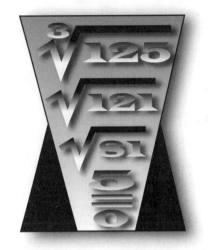

ACTIVITY 154 Solving Equations

Name:_____

Date:_____

Decide where to put parentheses, if necessary, and in what order to do each operation. Solve for n.

1. $6n - \frac{3}{4} \cdot 17 - 6 = 0$ $n =$ _____

2. $3 n \cdot n - 16 \div 2 = 13$ $n =$ _____

3. $63 \cdot 10^3 \div 7 \cdot 45 \div 5 = n$ $n =$ _____

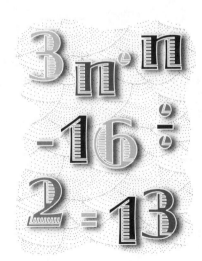

ACTIVITY 155 Solving Equations

Name:_____

Date:_____

Find all values for *n* in each inequality.

1 $\dfrac{1}{10} \cdot 5^2 \le n \le \dfrac{3}{5} \cdot 3^2$ _____

2 $2^3 \cdot 10^2 \le n \le 4^3 \cdot (10^3 \div 10^1)$ _____

3 $[(17 \cdot \dfrac{2}{3}) - \dfrac{1}{3}] + 1 \le n$ _____

4. $\dfrac{1}{5} n \ge (4 \cdot \dfrac{8}{36})$ _____

ACTIVITY 156 Solving Equations

Name:_____

Date:_____

Insert the correct symbol in each equation. Choose either $\ge$ or $\le$.

1. $(-21) + 7 + (-2)$ _____ -6

2. $[13 - 5(2^2 - 3^0)]$ _____ 0

3. $5^{-3} \cdot 3^{-2}$ _____ $\dfrac{1}{5} \cdot 10^{-2}$

4. $(8^3 \cdot 2^2) \div 8^2$ _____ $5^0 \cdot (3^3 - 3^5)$

ACTIVITY 157 Solving Equations

Name: _____

Date: _____

Solve the equations using these values.

$$a = \frac{1}{3},\ b = 2,\ c = 3\frac{1}{2}$$

1. $a(bc - 5) =$ _____

2. $b^{-2} \cdot ac =$ _____

3. $2(bc - a) + 3 =$ _____

ACTIVITY 158 Solving Equations

Name: _____

Date: _____

Decide if each equation is possible or impossible.

1. $n^2 + 3 < 0$ Possible   Impossible

2. $7 < n < 3^{-2}$ Possible   Impossible

3. $4^4 \geq n \geq 2^8$ Possible   Impossible

4. $2(-9) \geq \sqrt{81} \cdot 2$ Possible   Impossible

5. $-6 \cdot (-7 - 4) > 8^2$ Possible   Impossible

ACTIVITY 159 Percent

Name:_____

Date:_____

Dotty's Discount Shop is featuring these sales this week:

Use what you know about percentages and proportions to find the rate of reduction on each item.

BIG SALE!	Regular Price:	Discounted price:
A dozen doughnuts	$ 4.50	$ 3.75
A dozen cases of detergent	$ 65.75	$ 46.69
A drum and drumsticks	$159.95	$126.00
Deep-sea diving gear	$529.99	$397.49

Which product has the greatest percentage of reduction? _____

ACTIVITY 160 Percent

Name:_____

Date:_____

Three actresses, Gretta, Loretta, and Marietta, spend various amounts of time in makeup. Which one spends the highest percent of her time there?

Calculate the percentage of time each actress spends in makeup.

	Time in Makeup	Total Work Time	Percent
1. Gretta	2 hours, 15 minutes	7 hours, 10 minutes	_____
2. Loretta	1 hour, 50 minutes	6 hours, 45 minutes	_____
3. Marietta	3 hours	10 hours, 12 minutes	_____

4. Who spends the highest percentage of her time in makeup? _____

ACTIVITY 161 Using Algebra With a Geometry Problem

Name:_____

Date:_____

A rectangle has a perimeter of 12 inches. The length is 1 inch longer than the width.

What are the dimensions of the rectangle?

1. Write an equation to help you solve the problem.

_____

2. Answer: $W =$ _____ $L =$ _____

$p = 12$

ACTIVITY 162 Using Algebra With a Geometry Problem

Name:_____

Date:_____

Each side of this square is 6 inches long. Assume that the sides on square B are half that long. Write an equation that will tell you the area of each of these shapes. Solve.

1. A: equation = _____

    area = _____

2. B: equation = _____

    area = _____

3. C: equation = _____

    area = _____

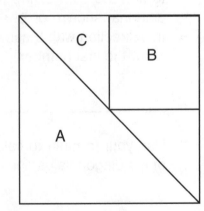

ACTIVITY 163 Using Algebra With Calendar Problems

Name:_____

Date:_____

Look at this calendar page.

1. Write an equation that tells how to find the sum of the numbers in the diagonal shown, or of any diagonal in this direction when you know the first number.

_____

2. Use your formula to calculate the sum of the diagonals beginning with

1 _____   2 _____

3 _____   4 _____

1	2	3	4	5	6	7
8	9	10	11	12	13	14
15	16	17	18	19	20	21
22	23	24	25	26	27	28
29	30	31				

3. What is the difference between each of your sums? _____ Why? _____

ACTIVITY 164 Using Algebra With Calendar Problems

Name:_____

Date:_____

1. Write an equation that tells you how to find the sum of the numbers in the diagonal shown, or of any diagonal in this direction with 5 numbers when you know the first number.

_____

2. Use your formula to calculate the sum of the diagonals beginning with

5 _____

6 _____

7 _____

1	2	3	4	5	6	7
8	9	10	11	12	13	14
15	16	17	18	19	20	21
22	23	24	25	26	27	28
29	30	31				

Answer Keys

LEVEL ONE

Activity 1 (p. 1)
1. subtract 8: 32; 24; 16; 8
2. multiply by 1, multiply by 2, multiply by 3...:
   168; 840; 5,040; 35,280
3. subtract 2, add 6, subtract 2, add 6...: 11; 17; 15; 21

Activity 2 (p. 1)
Arrangements will vary.
In **1.** these numbers will be opposite: 12–18, 13–17, 14–16.
In **2.** these numbers will be opposite: 7–23, 9–21, 11–19, 13–17.
In both **1.** and **2.**, the magic sum is 45.
3. Because the center number is the same.
4. The sum is 3 times the center number.

Activity 3 (p. 2)
1. y: 6, 13, 15; $x \div 6 = y$
2. y: 31, 23, 71; $2x + 1 = y$
3. y: 34, 58, 73; $3x - 2 = y$

Activity 4 (p. 2)
1. The final number is always 5 times the original number plus 1.
2. Start with A. Add 10 → A + 10; Multiply by 5 → 5(A + 10) = 5A + 50; Add 1 → 5A + 50 + 1; Subtract 50 → 5A + 1.

Activity 5 (p. 3)
June – 600, July – 700, Aug – 800, Sept – 900

Activity 6 (p. 3)
1. 28 2. 30 3. 32
4. Increasing the length by 1 m increases the perimeter by 2 m.
5. $2(L + W) = P$ 6. $2(L + 1 + W) = P + 2$

Activity 7 (p. 4)
1. D 2. A 3. B 4. E

Activity 8 (p. 4)
1. B, D 2. B, C

Activity 9 (p. 5)
At minutes 26–30, Mary will be typing 42 words per minute, for a total of 210 words in that 5-minute time period.

Activity 10 (p. 5)
One answer: Each day, Mama's Pizzeria sells twice as many cheese pizzas as pepperoni. Monday, she sold 5 pepperoni pizzas. The next four days, she sold one more pepperoni pizza than the night before. The table shows the number of pepperoni and cheese pizzas sold for the entire week. Title: Number of Pepperoni and Cheese Pizzas Sold at Mama's Pizzeria.

Activity 11 (p. 6)
The line is not straight because the rate of snow melt was not consistent.

Activity 12 (p. 6)
1. B 2. Word problems for Graph A will vary.

Activity 13 (p. 7)
Table: 21, 28, 35, 42

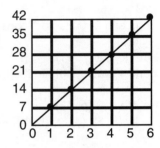

Activity 14 (p. 7)
Week 3 – 1″, Week 4 – 2″, Week 5 – 4″, Week 6 – 8″; It is not a straight line because the change varies.

Activity 15 (p. 8)
Savings increases in multiples of 3.

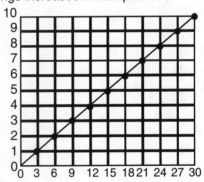

Activity 16 (p. 8)
Table: 30, 25, 15, 5, 0. 1. 16 2. It is constant.

Activity 17 (p. 9)
1. y: 5, 8, 11, 23 2. y is one less than three times x.
4. Yes 5. $3x - 1 = y$

Activity 18 (p. 9)
1. $A = l \cdot w$ 2. $P = 2l + 2w$
3. $\frac{1}{2} bh = A$ 4. $d = 2r$

Activity 19 (p. 10)
Variations are possible.
1. $1,876 - 938 = 938$ 2. $7,674 + 960 = 8,634$

Activity 20 (p. 10)
Variations are possible.
1. $8 \cdot x = 280$ **2.** $(60 \cdot 5) \div 24 = x$
3. $60 \text{ in.}^2 + (12 \cdot 3 \text{ in.}^2) = x$ **4.** $425 + (425 \cdot 0.30) = x$

Activity 21 (p. 11)
In all cases, it is possible to solve the problem without using variables. But it will be quicker to solve most of them with the help of variables.

On #3, instead of lengthy trial and error, you could simply use this equation:
Where g = the number of gold balloons, $g + 2g = 750$, so $3g = 750$ and $g = 250$. The store sold 250 gold balloons and 500 blue balloons.

Activity 22 (p. 11)
x and y match, both in the table and on the graph.

Activity 23 (p. 12)
(2, 4), (3, 6), (4, 8), (5, 10), (6, 12) Equation: $y = 2x$

Activity 24 (p. 12)
1. less steep **2.** less steep **3.** more steep

Activity 25 (p. 13)
Students' equations may vary.
1. $10 \cdot 4 = q$, 40 quarts
2. $10 \cdot (4 \cdot 2) = p$, 80 pints
3. $10 \cdot (4 \cdot 2 \cdot 2) = c$, 160 cups

Activity 26 (p. 13)
Students' equations may vary.
1. $1,760 \cdot 2 = y$, 3,520 yards
2. $(5,280 \cdot 2) \div 8 = f$, 1,320 feet
3. $(5,280 \cdot 12 \cdot 2) \div 3 = i$, 42,240 inches

Activity 27 (p. 14)
$0.30 \cdot C = i$
2. $42.60 **3.** 99 **4.** $130.50 **5.** 658

Activity 28 (p. 14)
Word problems will vary.
1. 10 **2.** 120 **3.** 5

Activity 29 (p. 15)
1. the number of Betsy's monkeys **2.** 17
3. Betsy: 17, Kelsie: 29

Activity 30 (p. 15)
1. $85x - 240 = y$ **2.** -$155 **3.** -$70 **4.** $15
5. $100 **6.** $185 **7.** Yes
8. There is a constant rate of change.

Activity 31 (p. 16)
Equations may vary.
1. $4 \cdot 60 = d$, $d = 240$ miles
2. $528 \div 12 = r$, $r = 44$ mph
3. $17,222 \cdot 24 = d$, $d = 413,328$ miles
4. $4,590 \div 510 = t$, $t = 9$ hours

Activity 32 (p. 16)
1. $3 \cdot 90 = d$, $d = 270$ miles
2. $3,960 \div 8 = r$, $r = 495$ mph
3. The zebra wins. It takes him just 30 minutes to run 20 miles, so he gets to the water at 11:30, the same time the cheetah is leaving.
4. $0.2 \cdot 24 = d$, $d = 4.8$ miles

Activity 33 (p. 17)
1. $r \cdot 4 = 36$ **2.** $r = 9$ m.p.h.

Activity 34 (p. 17)
Gary: $65 \cdot t = 130$, $t = 2$ hours. Gary will arrive at 11 A.M.
Ann: $40 \cdot t = 60$, $t = 1.5$.

Ann needs to leave $1\frac{1}{2}$ hours before 11 A.M., or at 9:30 A.M.

Activity 35 (p. 18)
1. A **2.** A. 36 B. 4 C. j
3. Any equation in this form: $(x + y) + z = x + (y + z)$

Activity 36 (p. 18)
1. C **2.** Any equation in this form: $2(x + y) = 2x + 2y$
3. Any equation in this form: $(x \cdot y) \cdot z = x \cdot (y \cdot z)$

Activity 37 (p. 19)
1. b **2.** a, b, c **3.** b, c **4.** a, b **5.** c

Activity 38 (p. 19)
1. $3(4 + 10) = Y$
$3 \cdot 14 = Y$
$42 = Y$

2. $3(\frac{1}{2} + 6) = Y$
$3(6\frac{1}{2}) = Y$
$19.5 = Y$

3. $3(1.5 + -3) = Y$
$3(-1.5) = Y$
$-4.5 = Y$

Activity 39 (p. 20)
1. $4(3 \cdot 2 - 1) + 5 = Y$
$4(6 - 1) + 5 = Y$
$4(5) + 5 = Y$
$20 + 5 = Y$
$25 = Y$

2. $4(\frac{1}{2} \cdot 8 - 1) + 5 = Y$
$4(4 - 1) + 5 = Y$
$4(3) + 5 = Y$
$12 + 5 = Y$
$17 = Y$

3. $4(20 \cdot 0.5 - 1) + 5 = Y$
$4(10 - 1) + 5 = Y$
$4(9) + 5 = Y$
$36 + 5 = Y$
$41 = Y$

Activity 40 (p. 20)

1. $(2 \cdot 5 + 3 \cdot 6) - 7 = n$ **2.** $n = [(5 \cdot 7) \div 5] \cdot 6$
$(10 + 18) - 7 = n$ $n = (35 \div 5) \cdot 6$
$28 - 7 = n$ $n = 7 \cdot 6$
$21 = n$ $n = 42$

3. $(9 \cdot 6) - (4 \cdot 7) = n \div 5$
$54 - 28 = n \div 5$
$26 = n \div 5$
$5 \cdot 26 = n$
$130 = n$

Activity 41 (p. 21)
Variations are possible.
1. $3 \cdot (18 \div 3)$ **2.** $(5 \div 5) + 24$ **3.** $(4 \cdot 18) \div 2$
4. $(10 \div 5) - 2$ **5.** $(120 \div 2) + (4 \cdot 10)$
6. $(4 \cdot 3) \cdot (16 \div 2)$

Activity 42 (p. 21)
Answers will vary. One possible answer for each is given.
1. $(72 + 12) - 60 = 24$ **2.** $7 + [(7 + 8) \div 3] = 12$
3. $(44 \div 4) + (2 \cdot 3) = 17$ **4.** $(10 \div 10) - 10 = \text{-}9$
5. $(5 \cdot 5) + (5 \cdot 5) = 50$

Activity 43 (p. 22)

1. $2y - 6 = 12 + 6$ **2.** $\dfrac{48}{3} = \dfrac{3(n \cdot 4)}{3}$
$\dfrac{2y}{2} = \dfrac{18}{2}$ $\dfrac{16}{4} = \dfrac{n \cdot 4}{4}$
$y = 9$ $4 = n$

3. $8n - (9 \cdot 3) = 45$
$8n - 27 = 45 + 27$
$\dfrac{8n}{8} = \dfrac{72}{8}$
$n = 9$

Activity 44 (p. 22)

1. $9n + (5 \div 5) = 1$ **2.** $3n = 42 - (6 \cdot 6)$
$9n + 1 = 1 - 1$ $3n = 42 - 36$
$\dfrac{9n}{9} = \dfrac{0}{9}$ $\dfrac{3n}{3} = \dfrac{6}{3}$
$n = 0$ $n = 2$

3. $n + 11 = 3(14 \div 2)$
$n + 11 = 3 \cdot 7$
$n + 11 - 11 = 21 - 11$
$n = 10$

Activity 45 (p. 23)

1. $H > \frac{1}{2} \cdot 6{,}129{,}000$ **2.** $W < \frac{1}{3} \cdot 2{,}436{,}000$
$H > 3{,}064{,}500$ $W < 812{,}000$
Harriet must get more than 3,064,500 votes.
Winslow received less than 812,000 votes.

Activity 46 (p. 23)
1. $n > 42$ **2.** $50 > n$ **3.** $100 < n$

Activity 47 (p. 24)
1. 10, 13, 16, 19, 22, 25, 28, 31   **2.** 46, 301
3. Where s is the number of squares, $(s \cdot 3) + 1$

Activity 48 (p. 24)
On Day 7, Ryan will have $3.15 more than Reta.

| | Ryan | | Reta | | Difference in Value |
Day	# of Nickels	Value of Nickels	# of Dimes	Value of Dimes	
1	25	$1.25	8	$0.80	$0.45
2	50	$2.50	16	$1.60	$0.90
3	75	$3.75	24	$2.40	$1.35
4	100	$5.00	32	$3.20	$1.80
5	125	$6.25	40	$4.00	$2.25
6	150	$7.50	48	$4.80	$2.70
7	175	$8.75	56	$5.60	$3.15
8	200	$10.00	64	$6.40	$3.60

Activity 49 (p. 25)
Approximate values are shown on the graph.
1. 1.75
2. 2.25
3. 2.6

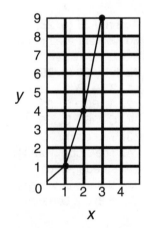

Activity 50 (p. 25)
Thursday, as shown on graph.

—— Annie's Antiques

- - - - - Zany Zithers

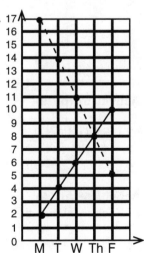

Activity 51 (p. 26)
$(W - E) \div 5 = S$;
1. $(325 - 10) \div 5 = 63$ **2.** $(452 - 22) \div 5 = 86$
3. $(400 - 5) \div 5 = 79$ **4.** $(433 - 13) \div 5 = 84$

Activity 52 (p. 26)
$[(W - 1) \cdot 7] + D = C$

Activity 53 (p. 27)
1. a. 10   b. 20   c. 30
2. 10 sq. ft./hour
3. 5 hours
4. 120 sq. ft.

Activity 54 (p. 27)
6 F.A.T. burgers

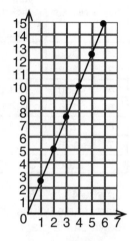

Activity 55 (p. 28)
60 workers are needed.

Activity 56 (p. 28)
1. $3S = P$
2. A. 30   B. 33
    C. 36   D. 39
3. See graph.
4. The slope would be
    steeper, because the
    change in *y* is greater
    with the squares.

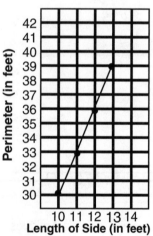

Perimeter (in feet)

10 11 12 13 14
Length of Side (in feet)

LEVEL TWO

Activity 57 (p. 29)
1. 1.8 ($\cdot$ 2, + 3, - 4, $\cdot$ 2, + 3, - 4 ...)
2. 15.8 (+ 1.3, $\cdot$ 2, + 1.3, $\cdot$ 2 ...)
3. 4.5 ($\div$ 2, + 2, $\cdot$ 2, $\div$ 2, + 2, $\cdot$ 2 ...)
4. 3.1 (+ 0.7, + 0.7, - 0.4, - 0.4 ...)

Activity 58 (p. 29)
A. Each number is the sum of the two directly above it.
7   1   7   21   35   35   21   7   1
8 1   8   28   56   70   56   28   8   1
9 1 9   36   84   126 126   84   36 9   1

Activity 59 (p. 30)
1. 9 years old   **2.** 33 minutes
3. 120 pounds less each hour

Activity 60 (p. 30)
1. The fine is 15¢ a day for each of the first 6 days. For
    days 7–15, the fine is 23¢ a day. For days over 15,
    the fine is 35¢ a day.
2. (6 days $\cdot$ 0.15) + (2 days $\cdot$ 0.23) = $1.36
3. (6 days $\cdot$ 0.15) + (9 days $\cdot$ 0.23) + (14 days $\cdot$ 0.35)
    = $7.87

Activity 61 (p. 31)
The sales for odd-numbered days increase by 50 books
each day. The sales for even-numbered days decrease
by 10.

Activity 62 (p. 31)
D   Waverly   7:30 A.M.   Willis   8:00 A.M.
E   Valley   8:10 A.M.   Velour   8:45 A.M.
F   Umber   8:55 A.M.   Upton   9:35 A.M.

Activity 63 (p. 32)
2, 3, 4, 6 are true.

Activity 64 (p. 32)
1. matches the graph. When the pattern is extended,
    Oct. shows 90¢, Nov. is 80¢, and Dec. is 90¢.

Activity 65 (p. 33)
1. 18 cm   **2.** 22 cm   **3.** 42 cm   **4.** 202 cm
5. The perimeter is the number of hexagons multi-
    plied by 4, plus 2.   **6.** $(h \cdot 4) + 2 = p$

Activity 66 (p. 33)
1. 10   **2.** 15   **3.** 21   **4.** 28
5. The number of segments increases by 1, 2, 3, 4, 5,...

Activity 67 (p. 34)
1. c   **2.** a   **3.** e   **4.** d

Activity 68 (p. 34)
1. $\frac{1}{3}(13 + 23) = n$ **2.** $\frac{1}{4}n = 90$ **3.** $0.2(65 - 27) = n$
4. $0.56 \div (0.3 \cdot 8) = n$ **5.** $n = 9 + (\frac{1}{2} \cdot 32)$

Activity 69 (p. 35)
$6(\frac{3}{4}) + 8(\frac{1}{2}) + x(\frac{1}{4}) \geq 10$, $x \geq 6$

Activity 70 (p. 35)
Sun – 120, Mon – 155, Tue – 180, Wed – 200,
Thu – 240, Fri – 245, Sat – 320

Activity 71 (p. 36)
1. $37.80, $34.02, $30.62, $27.56, $24.80, $22.32
2. $42.42, $42.84, $43.27, $43.70, $44.14, $44.58

Activity 72 (p. 36)
1, 2, 4, and **5** are all possible. **3** is not.

Activity 73 (p. 37)
The snail finishes first, at 1:12.
The turtle would finish at almost 1:14.

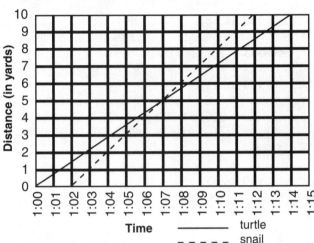

Time ——— turtle
      - - - - snail

Activity 74 (p. 37)
Table: 2.25, 4.5, 6.75, 9.0, 11.25, 13.5
1. $3L = P$ **2.** yes   **3.** yes

Activity 75 (p. 38)
The cats will meet after 16 minutes, 24 feet off the ground.

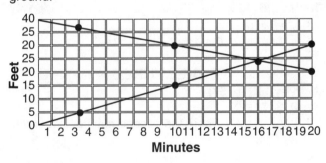

Activity 76 (p. 38)
6.6, 8.8, 11, 13.2; Equation: $x \cdot 2.2 = y$

Activity 77 (p. 39)
Tables: **1.** 5, 9, 13, 17, 21   **2.** 4, 9, 16, 25, 36
3. 1. is the linear function.

Activity 78 (p. 39)
Tables will vary. Only **1.** is a linear function.

Activity 79 (p. 40)
1. 4; 1; 4   **2.** 1; 1; 1   **3.** 1; 3; $\frac{1}{3}$

Activity 80 (p. 40)
1. 6.28, 9.42, 12.56, 15.7, 18.84.
2. Linear   **4.** 3.14.

Activity 81 (p. 41)
Table: -4, -2, 0, 2, 4;   **3.** 2   **4.** -6

Activity 82 (p. 41)
Table: 0, $\frac{1}{2}$, 1, $1\frac{1}{2}$, 2, $2\frac{1}{2}$, 3   **3.** 0.5 or $\frac{1}{2}$ **4.** 0

Activity 83 (p. 42)
1. 0, 2   **2.** 2, -4   **3.** -1, 2

Activity 84 (p. 42)
1. C   **2.** D   **3.** E   **4.** A   **5.** B

Activity 85 (p. 43)
1. $x = 744 \div 24$; $x = 31$
2. $(440 \cdot 1,760) \div 20 = x$; 38,720 yds. = x
3. $(14 \cdot 1,760) \cdot 2 = x$; 49,280 yds. = x

Activity 86 (p. 43)
1. a. $p = 5s$ **b.** 886   **c.** 174.1
2. a. $h = 7s$; $x = 3s$ **b.** 1.62   **c.** 10.5

Activity 87 (p. 44)
1. $[26 \cdot (14 - 2)] = x$; 312 = x
2. $[(12 \cdot 2) + (19 \cdot 2)] - (9 \cdot 2) = x$; 44 = x

Activity 88 (p. 44)
1. $0.4(20) = 1.6y$; $y = 5$ **2.** $26 + x^2 = 3^3$; $x = 1$
3. $5^3 - 44 = y^2$; $y = 9$

Activity 89 (p. 45)
$p = 50 - [(d \cdot 0.08) \cdot 50]$
For Day 3, $p = 38.

Activity 90 (p. 45)
Table: **2.** 13, 16; **3.** 19.5, 24
4. $s(6.5) + s(8) = 159.5$; $s = 11$

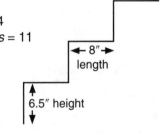

←— 8″ —→
length

↕ 6.5″ height

Activity 91 (p. 46)
1. $r \cdot \frac{1}{3}$ hr. = 15 mi.; $r = 45$ m.p.h.
2. 15 m.p.h. $\cdot t = 20$ mi.; $t = 1\frac{1}{3}$ hr. The bicyclist would arrive $1\frac{1}{3}$ hr. after he began, or at 3:20 P.M.
3. $r \cdot \frac{3}{4}$ hr. = 20 mi. + 15 mi. + 12 mi.; $r = \cancel{62.67\ \text{m.p.h.}}$

$\frac{47}{\frac{3}{4}}$ 56 mph

Activity 92 (p. 46)
1. 3 lb./min • 60 min = 180 lb.
2. 2 lb./min • 60 min = 120 lb.
3. 1.5 lb./min • 60 min = 90 lb. **4.** Stanley

Activity 93 (p. 47)
1. 9 A.M. **2.** 120,000 miles

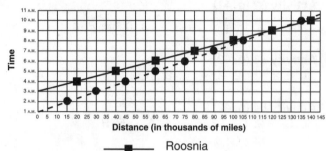

Roosnia
Hoosnia

Activity 94 (p. 47)
A's steam reaches the water first, at 10 A.M. The steam from B reaches it at 10:15.

Activity 95 (p. 48)
1, 4, 5

Activity 96 (p. 48)
2, 5

Activity 97 (p. 49)
1. b, c **2.** b **3.** a, c **4.** b, c **5.** a

Activity 98 (p. 49)
1. b **2.** a, c **3.** c **4.** a, c **5.** b, c

Activity 99 (p. 50)
1. 25 **2.** 915 **3.** -2,709

Activity 100 (p. 50)
1. 26 **2.** 13.5 **3.** $4\frac{3}{4}$

Activity 101 (p. 51)
1. 5 **2.** 17 **3.** -10

Activity 102 (p. 51)
1. $n = 5$ **2.** $n = 84$

Activity 103 (p. 52)
1. $n = 72$ **2.** $n = 43$

Activity 104 (p. 52)
1. $(56 - 4^2) + 3^2$ **2.** $(6^3 \div 6^1) • 10^2$
3. $25 \div [(15 - 10) • (8 - 7)]$ **4.** $\left(\frac{1}{3} • \frac{1}{4}\right) + \left(\frac{3}{4} - \frac{1}{4}\right)$
5. $[(10^4 • 10^2) \div 10^3] + 10^2$

Activity 105 (p. 53)
1. $n - 5 < (9 • 7) - (6 \div 3)$; $n < 50$
2. $\frac{1}{2}n + [(64 \div 8) - 2] > 10$; $n > 8$

Activity 106 (p. 53)
1. $n > 33$ **2.** $7\frac{1}{3} > n$

Activity 107 (p. 54)
11 dividers

Activity 108 (p. 54)
1. A **2.** months 2 to 4 **3.** the first 2 months
4. $60,000 **5.** $70,000
   $70,000

Activity 109 (p. 55)
1. $1,000 + [(0.065 • 1,000) • 5] = n$; $n = \$1,325$
2. $n(0.065 • 1,000) \geq 1,500$; $n \geq 23.08$ In 23 years, Beth will have earned $1,495. In 24 years, the interest is $1,560.

Activity 110 (p. 55)
$(110 • 20) + (215 • 10) + (n • 5) \leq 5,000$, $n \leq 130$ $5 bills

Activity 111 (p. 56)
Table: 4 cm − 64, 8; 5 cm − 125, 8; 6 cm − 216, 8.
1. $s^3 = c$
2. The graph produces a straight line, slope is 0.

Activity 112 (p. 56)
1.–2. Answers will vary.
Table: 126, 120, 110, 96
4. $b = 16$, $h = 16$
5. Either $b = 1$, $h = 31$, or $b = 31$, $h = 1$.

LEVEL THREE

Activity 113 (p. 57)
1. 2, 3, 7, 11
2. Look at rows where the second number is a prime number.

Activity 114 (p. 57)
1. the 2nd row and the 8th row **2.** 16th
3. The rows are all powers of 2: $2^0 =$ 1st row, $2^1 =$ 2nd row, $2^2 =$ 4th row, and so on.

Activity 115 (p. 58)
1. $\frac{20}{27}, \frac{20}{81}, \frac{20}{243}$ **2.** 9, 27, 54
3. 6.3, 7.2, 8.3 **4.** $9\frac{1}{16}, 9\frac{1}{32}, 9\frac{1}{64}$